CULTIVATE
THE PROCESS OF LIVING FROM YOUR HEART

cultivate
cul·ti·vate \ˈkəl-tə-ˌvāt\

: to prepare and use for the raising of crops
: to loosen or break up the soil
: to foster the growth of
: to improve by labor, care or study
: further, encourage
: to seek the society of
: make friends with

IN THESE PAGES, YOU WILL FIND STORIES AND TEACHINGS THAT CONNECT TO OUR COMMUNITY'S HONEST JOURNEY WITH GOD. OUR DESIRE IS THAT YOU WOULD ENGAGE EACH WRITING WITH YOUR WHOLE HEART AND DO THE WORK IT REQUIRES TO CULTIVATE A *THRIVING RELATIONSHIP* WITH THE FATHER, SON AND HOLY SPIRIT. MANY OF THESE ARTICLES END WITH A PROMPT TO JOURNAL THE VOICE OF THE LORD. JESUS SAYS IN JOHN 10:27, *"MY SHEEP HEAR MY VOICE,* AND I KNOW THEM, AND THEY FOLLOW ME". AS A CHILD OF GOD, YOU HAVE ACCESS TO HIS VOICE, YOU CAN HEAR HIM, AND IT IS IMPORTANT THAT YOU RECORD, SAVOR AND DECLARE HIS THOUGHTS OVER YOUR LIFE. WHEN YOU JOURNAL HIS THOUGHTS, YOU WILL REMEMBER HOW DEEPLY HE LOVES YOU AND WHO YOU TRULY ARE. WE ENCOURAGE YOU TO *CENTER YOUR HEART* IN THIS SIMPLE TRUTH: GOD IS A LOVING FATHER, READY AND EAGER TO SPEAK TO YOU.

TABLE *of* CONTENTS

02.
COMMUNICATION
valuing others through words, time and effort

01.
SELF-AWARENESS
valuing yourself the way God values you

03.
GENEROSITY
letting your love overflow into the world around you

01.

10 IT'S NOT A COMPETITION
12 VULNERABILITY
18 WHAT KILLS CONNECTION
22 WINDOWS AND DOORS
26 LEAST OF THESE
28 TWO-WAY STREET
30 GIVING IN TO TEAM
32 PASSIVITY
34 THE NEW GUY
37 GRIEF'S TERRAIN
40 UNDER NEW MANAGEMENT
42 THE HONESTY TOOL
48 LAND IN GRATITUDE
49 MEASUREMENT
50 OPPOSITES ATTRACT
54 APPLES AND ORANGES
56 SPHERES OF INFLUENCE
60 PEACEMAKING
62 REJECTING COMPARISON

02.

66 VALUES
70 STYLES OF COMMUNICATION
78 THE COMMUNICATION TOOL
86 THE FRIEND-LEADER DYNAMIC
90 JOYFUL WORK
93 TELEPHONE
94 PAST SOCIAL PROTOCOL
96 MISTAKES
102 SHARING SPACES
104 ASKING FOR HELP
106 SPEAKING INTO PEOPLE'S LIVES
108 COMMUNITY CULTURE

03.

113 RANGE OF COLOR
116 EVERY LITTLE THING
118 GOLD RUSH
122 THE GRATITUDE TOOL
126 EVERY SOUL AN AVENUE
128 WHEN GOD COMES TO COOK
132 BECAUSE OF LOVE
134 EXTRAVAGANCE
136 GIFT OF TEARS
138 LOVING THE WORLD AROUND YOU
142 TO THE ENDS OF THE EARTH
144 THE TABLE WHERE COMMUNITY FEASTS
148 THE ART OF NEIGHBORING
152 THE FRUIT LADY
154 A WAR OF BLESSING

A NOTE FROM THE EDITOR

here's to THE REWARD OF LOVING

by MELISSA HELSER

WE HAD JUST FINISHED LEADING WORSHIP, AND OUT OF THE CORNER OF MY EYE, I SAW A MAN SITTING ON THE FRONT ROW.

A man Jonathan and I had connection with years before. My heart jumped at the chance to see him again. I tapped him on the shoulder, and a huge smile filled both of our faces. Oh, the beauty of fathers in the faith. I sat down next to him and felt the gift of the presence of someone who really sees me. He looked me in the eyes and affirmed everything we were putting our hands to. He encouraged the new songs we had written, our growing community and the discipleship school we'd started. He said, "I've heard so many amazing things. I am so proud of you guys." I felt the presence of the Heavenly Father as I received the encouragement, like water to my soul. We were in our early thirties and ten years into camps, schools and pioneering a community, as well as raising children, traveling and leading worship. Affirmation from a father in the faith could not have come at a better time. He looked at me and said, "Can I give you some advice?" I smiled and said, "Absolutely, please speak into anything." He said, "People will come to you and ask for your model. They will want to replicate what you've done. But these things can't be replicated. Don't give people your model. Give them your values. What are the foundations you're building everything on? You can reproduce values anywhere." I knew in that moment that God Himself was giving Jonathan and me a compass, that would prove over and over to be tried and true. I left feeling like I had just been given the deepest nugget of wisdom.

We are now ten years past that moment and finally ready to offer our values to you, the reader. Community is messy and hard. Commitment to people has to go beyond what feels good. It takes a ton of work. There are communities all over the world that will have different models for how they work things out, and a different set of values. We are only one expression: a community with a mission of discipleship and raising up whole creatives. This book is not about how to build community. It is about The Art of Connection. It is the deeper value system of loving people well. Every family, church, business and relationship has a spoken or unspoken set of values. Our hope is that this volume of *Cultivate* would inspire and teach you how to do your relationships really well. In Volume V, we focused on marriage, dating, parenting and relating to your parents after you're an adult. Now we are going to go broader, to your friendships, your co-working relationships, your team, the stranger at the local coffee shop, essentially to the world around you. What does The Art of Connection look like with people you don't have a covenant relationship with? What does it look like to fight for connection in conflict? What are the value systems that keep our community going? We constantly change our model, reform our school rhythms and shift our work flow. Our values keep us anchored in the *why* we do what we do. They are the fuel for the work it takes to keep unity without control and to fight for connection without striving. My prayer

photograph by MORGAN CAMPBELL

is that you find inspiration in these pages for how to love well, even when it costs you something.

When I think about our deepest core value, it would absolutely be to love the way that Jesus loved. Jonathan and I realized very quickly that to accomplish this, it was going to require a lot of work. We decided that we were worth the work and the reward of pressing into people, both when it's easy and when it's hard. We've looked to the way Jesus modeled healthy boundaries, confrontation and a laying down of His life for the world. He was a lover of people. And that love is incredibly challenging to our cultural norm.

I am a lover of tools. Garden tools, kitchen tools, really any tool that will make any job more efficient and bring a better outcome. I remember the moment I got a fancy apple peeler. You know, the ones that spin the apple in a circle and core it, peel it and cut it into a thin spiral of apple goodness. I can clearly remember the delight that I felt knowing that there was no way I could have accomplished the outcome without that amazing piece of equipment. I remember when we had enough money to buy a leaf blower. All of a sudden, the work of sweeping and raking our porches and yard got a lot easier and a lot more fun. It was still work but the outcome had a different reward. I tell my students, retreat guests or anyone I am counseling that I would never ask them to go into our garden and dig a hole with their bare hands. I would first teach them to use a shovel properly, and then ask them to dig a hole. So many of us have the belief that we're either good at relationships or not, good at communication or not, that we either have a desire for extravagance and generosity or we don't. I believe that everything in life has to be taught. And taught well. For Jonathan and me, it was a very natural thing to seek out and develop tools for emotional health. We wanted to go beyond giving people just an experience of our culture at our schools, camps and retreats. We wanted them to be taught how to steward the garden of their hearts every day, to find values that work and create culture wherever they are. This book is *full* of tools. Tried and true processes that will help you learn to do your relationships really well. These are tools we have developed over years of working them out in community, work, ministry, marriage, friendships and parenting. Our life isn't perfect and our relationships are not perfect. But we know what to do when it gets hard and we know how to intentionally cultivate the beauty we long to have.

I pray you pick up this book and do the work. For yourself, for the people you love and for the world around you. For your everyday life and for the legacy you're leaving on the earth. We are the light carriers. We are the culture shifters. If we won't do the work, who will? May you feel inspired and deeply challenged. Here's to changing your lineage and getting used to the reward of loving.

SECTION 01

SELF AWARENESS

"THE PURPOSES OF A PERSON'S HEART ARE DEEP WATERS, BUT ONE WHO HAS INSIGHT DRAWS THEM OUT."
PROVERBS 20:5

IT'S NOT A COMPETITION

From the first day of my marriage,

I was focused on being the best husband I could possibly be. I can be a very driven person at times, especially when I have a goal or a project to complete. This is usually a positive trait, but when projects become more important than people, it can produce a lot of damage. From our pre-marriage counseling, I took away the principle that to be a great husband, I needed to put God first and seek Him first before all things. My formula to achieve this success was to make sure I woke up early enough each morning to have at least a forty-five minute "quiet time" with God before I began the day. A couple of months into our marriage, I thought I was doing a wonderful job implementing this discipline into my life, but there was a big problem underneath the surface.

by JONATHAN DAVID HELSER
photograph by MORGAN CAMPBELL & SYDNEE MELA

Pride and judgment were growing in my heart towards Melissa. See, I had noticed that Melissa was not as disciplined as I was in having her quiet times each morning. Instead of delighting in my time with God, it had secretly become this competition of proving how much better I was than Melissa.

After several weeks of this self-righteous judgment building in my heart, I had a life-changing moment with God. I had woken up early one morning and it was another day when Melissa didn't wake up as early as me. I was finishing up my time with the Lord when I heard Him speak very clearly, "Jonathan, thank you so much for giving me your time this morning." I instantly responded back to Him, "No problem, God. I know how important this is." Then with such a deep kindness, the Lord said to me, "Jonathan, you give me forty-five minutes each day, but Melissa gives me the whole day. You approach me as a duty to check off your list, but Melissa approaches me as a friend she is delighted to spend her whole life with."

I would love to see a slow-motion instant replay of my reaction when God spoke these words. The sword of God's kind correction went deep into my heart. As much as it hurt my pride that morning, the truth began to set me free and transform me. In that season of our lives, Melissa and I worked together every day. I began to watch her and notice how much she truly did practice the presence of God throughout her entire day. The area where I noticed the greatest contrast between the way she and I were doing life was how we interacted with people. Many times, I could be short or rude with our team because of how focused I was on completing projects, whereas Melissa saw the person before the project and walked in so much kindness with our team. I was in such a rush to do my job the best I could that I was actually missing the best thing: God's presence in the people all around me. During that season, I remember reading the words of I John 4:20-21. It was like the words were leaping off the page and cutting deep into my heart. It says that, "If you don't love a brother or sister, whom you can see, how can you truly love God, whom you can't see? For he has given us this command: whoever loves God must also demonstrate love to others" (TPT). I had read those verses many times, but now I realized that I was not fully living them. This gentle and firm correction from the Lord changed everything for me. It exposed the places of pride in my heart that were breaking my connection with God and other people. I had turned my relationship with God into a competition and I was missing the whole point of friendship.

When we compare and compete with others for our worth, we break connection. We become the judge and we miss out on the gift of true relationship. The first relationship in history that had a broken connection was between the two brothers Cain and Abel. The story goes that they brought God their offerings and God had favor on the younger brother, Abel's offering. Cain took offense at this and jealousy began to grow in his heart. God comes to the troubled Cain to help him like a loving Father, but Cain would not listen. I believe that God's desire was for the older brother to learn from his younger brother, but Cain's comparison grew into jealousy and anger that led to a terrible end to their brotherhood. What if Cain could have received the correction from the Father and

THERE IS A VAST CONTRAST BETWEEN THE POSTURE OF COMPARING OURSELVES TO OTHERS AND THE HUMBLE POSTURE OF LEARNING FROM ONE ANOTHER.

learned from his brother? What if he could have let go of the need to compare and compete, and built a connection with his brother instead of breaking it? When we choose to compare ourselves with others, we choose a cold, isolated prison of pride. But when we choose to learn from each other, the door of humility opens and leads us into extraordinary freedom and abundant life. There is a vast contrast between the posture of comparing ourselves to others and the humble posture of learning from one another. I believe that one of the greatest ways to cultivate the art of connection is found when we learn from one another.

There is another story of siblings in the Scriptures that highlights this thread of competition and how it robs us of connection. In Luke 10:38-42 (NIV), Jesus came to the home of the two sisters, Mary and Martha. "Martha was distracted by all the preparations that had to be made. She came to Him and asked, 'Lord, don't you care that my sister has left me to do the work by myself? Tell her to help me!' 'Martha, Martha,' the Lord answered, 'You are worried and upset about many things, but few things are needed—or indeed only one. Mary has chosen what is better, and it will not be taken away from her.'" Martha thought that she was giving Jesus what He wanted, but her project became more important than the presence of the King who was in her home. She was working with all her might to give Him the perfect meal, but what He desired was the connection that Mary's heart had chosen. I can clearly see myself in the hurry and the worry in Martha's heart. Both of these stories have broken my heart in the best way. They have been like a mirror to help me recognize how comparison breaks my connection with God and with those around me. I am provoked by the beautiful correction Jesus gave to Martha; to learn from those around me, to lay down my competition and discover what true connection is.

Prompt: Take a few moments to re-read the story in Luke 10:38-42. As you read, ask the Holy Spirit to search your heart and know you. Welcome God's correction into your life. Remember that correction is not punishment, but God's gift that we might be free and more fruitful. When you finish the story, take inventory of your relationships and ask God if there are any places where connection is being broken by competition and comparison. If He highlights an area, simply repent and then ask Him what you can learn from the person you've been comparing yourself to. Humble your heart in His presence and learn from those God has placed in your life.

vulnerability

by MELISSA HELSER

photography by MORGAN CAMPBELL

Sometimes I don't know why I choose to write about certain topics. I say in the planning session, "Yes! I have so much to write about when it comes to vulnerability." Then the deadlines come and go and I'm left swirling around a million thoughts in so many directions. I feel like I am standing in the middle of an intersection with twenty different roads to go down. It's not that I have nothing to write; I just have too much to write. Where do I even start? I could talk about vulnerability in marriage and how it's changed the way Jonathan and I relate to each other. Or the power of vulnerability in parenting, teaching our children to shed the layers of performance and perfectionism for a life of true strength. Or maybe the road of chronic illness; over twenty years of not getting to choose vulnerability, but it being forced on me. I've had to ask for help over and over, even when I just wanted to do it myself. Or maybe I could talk about full-time ministry…pastoring, leading a community, pioneering discipleship schools, retreats, camps, traveling the world and leading worship. Laying down my life for people that sometimes get it and sometimes don't.

This is what I know: Life is impossible to do without vulnerability.

What does it mean to be vulnerable?

One definition of vulnerability is: "Helpless, defenseless, powerless, weak. The quality or state of being exposed to the possibility of being attacked or harmed, either physically or emotionally."[1]

I know what you're thinking…*Forget it. That is not what I signed up for. Who wants to be helpless, defenseless, powerless?* Nobody! We want to be put together; powerful. We want to outgrow our need and present ourselves to the world as mature Christians lacking nothing. The only problem with this is that life is hard, relationships are hard. Marriage and parenting are hard. We can't work our way out of needing help and we certainly can't mature our way into independence. In the Kingdom it's the opposite. Everything is upside down. We mature into neediness, dependency. I absolutely love that the dictionary says, "The *quality* of being exposed to the *possibility* of harm." The quality…does that mean this is a good thing? Do we want to possess that quality? When I think about relationships and I read this definition, I begin to understand why it's so costly. Why so many of us refuse to engage in it. If we give in, we open ourselves to the possibility of pain.

When I think about Jesus, I am overcome at His willingness to be vulnerable. I am overcome at His intention to choose friends that He knew would end up denying their friendship, denying that they even knew Him, betraying Him to His face. I like to think of the moment at the last meal He had with His dearest friends. The eye contact He made with Judas all night. The internal prayers He must have prayed for

him. He was sitting close to Judas, close enough for them both to put their hands in the bowl of oil at the same time. When you are with your closest friends you can say a lot without speaking. I imagine there was a lot being said up until the moment that Jesus released him to do what he was going to do. And what about the next moments of Jesus in the garden at His deepest time of grief and sorrow and letting Himself *need His friends?* He needed them so much He kept going back to ask them to stay awake and pray for Him. This is our Savior, letting Himself be weak, letting Himself need.

Every part of my life has taught me something about being vulnerable. And every part of my life has challenged me to practice it. I remember the drive to her first horseback lesson. She was ten years old, sweet, quiet and showing excitement in her own way. Our drives then were always pretty quiet. Very different from my drives with my oldest son that were full of breathless conversations. Haven was different and I loved it. As an extrovert, I have embraced learning and loving parenting an introvert. We sat quietly and then I asked her, "Are you excited?" She replied, "Yes, I hope I find a best friend." I sat surprised, thinking to myself, *Does she realize this is a private lesson? It's just her and the instructor.* I tenderly told her, "Darling, it's a private lesson. There won't be other children there." She looked at me, clearly annoyed, and said, "I meant a horse, Mom!" That's when I knew I still had a lot to learn.

Four years later, she has completely fallen in love with riding. A love that has matured her deeply. She is now old enough and experienced enough to lease a horse. That is a big deal. It means she can go to the barn and ride whenever she wants to, and she can choose a horse to really bond with instead of riding a different horse every lesson. To my surprise she chose a small, stout Norwegian Fjord. A dusty-white horse that had just come to the barn from a former owner, who had left him in a field for seven years and never rode him. His name is Halvar. Haven is very tall for her age, and I was sure she would choose one of the huge thoroughbreds that she looked so majestic on. But no, she chose the smallest horse at the barn. Halvar is a unique horse—old, peculiar and a bit funny at times. But Haven loved him right away. She loved the challenge of teaching him new things and she especially loved how her instructors thought the world of her and how well she rode him. We went from lessons with a teacher to being alone at the barn with him. Just Haven, Halvar and me. I would love to interject here that I know nothing about horses or riding, I am just an innocent bystander.

The days started out amazing and then, slowly over two months, got harder and harder. He wouldn't listen. He pressed the boundaries. He slowed down when he was supposed to speed up and would speed up when he was supposed to slow down. He left Haven feeling defeated. Oftentimes, tears would come. What she thought leasing was going to be like ended up being very different. She thought she was ready to be in control. To be alone. To do it by herself. Oftentimes we perform for ourselves the most. I'd ask her if she wanted me to call her teacher and ask for help. "No," she would say, "I can do it." Eventually we hit a breaking point, and I was watching all the fun get sucked out of her riding. The tone was changing from, "I can't wait to ride," to, "I am going to get him to do what I want today. I am in charge." As a mom of teenagers, I am learning to walk that very fine line of offering help and letting them figure it out. It is a dance, and both are valuable. I knew we had hit a threshold…*The threshold wasn't that she needed help, the threshold was that she didn't know how to ask for it with no shame.*

I have come to hate the shame that shuts all of us down from asking for help. The shame that lies to us and keeps us from taking the risk of feeling helpless. It's the defeating feeling that we couldn't pull it off. The voice that says, "Why can't I do this?" The problem

is, shame turns into pride, and let's be honest: No one wants to admit that they don't really know what they're doing. There is a mentality we often operate in that says, *I'm just going to do this by myself, I don't want anyone to know, I'll just figure it out and then show the glossy version of myself.* How often are we unwilling to offer the broken parts of ourselves because of pride? What about the pride of the phrase, "I know?" I remember a moment with a student years ago who asked for help. She shared for a long time, and I gave her my thoughts only to the response of, " I know." I shared more thoughts and she just kept saying, "I know," over and over. Finally, I looked at her and said, "If you know so much, why did you ask for advice?" She looked at me, stunned and broke down crying. "Actually, I don't know. I need help," she replied through tears. At last, we had vulnerability. Pride and shame are not an adequate source of protection. Instead they keep us isolated and withhold the only thing that will draw us into safety, belonging and family. The beauty of feeling helpless is the reward of being met. It's the gift of knowing we aren't alone, the gift of *not* knowing the right thing to do. And it's true strength to fully embrace our neediness.

Safety is found first in Jesus. I've had to make it a priority to practice true vulnerability with the Lord first, letting the Holy Spirit speak truth into my life. Being helpless in the presence of the Father is one the most empowering things we can do. It has changed my life to pour my heart out to the Lord, and then do the most powerful act of vulnerability: stop, wait and listen to His voice. That might seem simple, but allowing the Lord or people to speak into our lives is really hard. Mostly because we all have something to prove. That moment of silence after you risk opening up, the moment you pause and let someone respond, the moment you say, "Help"—that is true vulnerability. And could it be that the pause is actually one of the most maturing things we can do? It's the courage to be helpless with no shame.

In my twenties, I thought I had vulnerability down pat. As an extrovert, I loved processing my life with others. I was open and honest. Talking about my struggles and mistakes was easy and effortless, as long as I tied everything up with a pretty bow: "...and now I'm okay!" But I was opening up in a way that left zero room for anyone to share their thoughts, feedback or wisdom. I started noticing that when I was was with Jonathan or my close friends, and I wanted to open up, I would fumble through my words and say things like, "I'm sorry, everything's actually okay," "I'm gonna be fine," or, "It's not a big deal." Shame. I didn't want to be helpless. I wanted to have it all together. I didn't want to ask for help, I wanted to already know it all. I wanted to figure it out by myself and then share my process. Pride.

I had to learn to let go of both streams of thought: shame and pride. I had to fully receive the gift of need. I decided to believe it was my honor to practice dependency, not my shame. I embraced the Jesus model. I learned to value my humanity instead of shaming it.

"He existed in the form of God, yet he gave no thought to seizing equality with God as his supreme prize. Instead he emptied himself of his outward glory by reducing himself to the form of a lowly servant. He became human! He humbled himself and became vulnerable, choosing to be revealed as a man and was obedient. He was a perfect example, even in his death—a criminal's death by crucifixion!" (Philippians 2:6-8, TPT).

She had been riding Halvar in circles for what felt like forever. As she passed me, I could see the tears streaming. It took a few minutes and then she finally rode up to the gate where I was. "Mom, I need help. I feel alone. This isn't what I thought it was going to be. I need my teacher to watch me. I don't know what to do. He won't listen to me." RELIEF. Finally we were opening up. Finally we were asking for help. Finally we were practicing vulnerability. I sighed, and looked her in the eyes. "This is really hard. I think you're right, we need help. First, let's invite the Holy Spirit to help us, and let's trade this pressure to perform for the joy of getting to ride. You don't have to know what to do." Tears streamed harder as she prayed her most honest prayer and released the shame and the pride to the Lord. The next day of riding wasn't perfect, but the pressure had lifted. And then out of nowhere, her teacher walked into the arena and said, "Haven, do you need help?" "Yes," she replied, with a look of relief and ecstatic joy that the Lord had answered her prayer so quickly. The gift of help is that someone can watch us and see the blind spots that are impossible for us to see. The shame lifted. She had nothing to prove and so much to learn. It wasn't perfect, but she wasn't alone. And that was the reward.

True vulnerability will swallow up the lie, "I have to do it alone." It knows that the risk will not be without pain and heartache, but the reward will be connection. The reward will be the gift of being seen, even in your mess and mostly in your need. The reward will be not having to fight all by yourself and isn't that what we all crave? To be fought for. To belong. To be known. My prayer is that you give in. Give in to being helpless. Give in to risking vulnerability in relationships even when you know it could cause pain. Give in to the maturing process of asking for help. It creates a strength in us, the glorious privilege as human beings to deeply need each other and to mostly need the Lord.

"Sweet friendships refresh the soul and awaken our hearts with joy, for good friends are like the anointing oil that yields the fragrant incense of God's presence." Proverbs 27:9, TPT

WHAT KILLS CONNECTION

by JESSIE MILLER —— artwork by JUSTINA STEVENS

Lasting friendships are meant to be fluid, full of movement and transitions. As feelings get hurt, expectations don't get met, new elements get added to your dynamic and old lies from the enemy rear their ugly heads, you can either run, hide or get honest. It's easy to let struggles lead us out of a friendship and misinterpret tension as a reason to "go our separate ways" either literally or internally. Yet, it is that very struggle to stay connected—that willingness of two people to lean into the Father and be vulnerable in the tension—that produces deep trust and a secure love that lasts. I have had the privilege of having friends in my life who have walked with me through many seasons—over a decade of changes. In order to keep these friends close, I have had to confront three main connection killers—comparison, assumption and performance—and instead embrace gratitude, vulnerability and trust.

COMPARISON

com·par·i·son | \ kəm-ˈper-ə-sən
: the representing of one thing or person as similar to or like another
: an examination of two or more items to establish similarities and dissimilarities

Comparison makes love brittle, quick to crack under the weight of any tension. It drains the joy of differences. What God offers us in a friend to inspire and help us, we perceive as a threat to our identity. *Oh, she is so good at talking to people. I'll never be like that.* These kinds of thoughts let your friends' strengths take away from your value and sow seeds of bitterness. What starts as comparison can quickly become resentment. *I like myself better when they aren't around.* The temptation is to handle these feelings by distancing yourself or competing—thus beginning a series of fruitless, painful actions. To keep a friend, you must instead embrace a humbling heart-shift towards gratitude. Gratitude breaks the spell of comparison. It helps you see all you have been given, instead of all you are lacking. Gratitude opens your eyes to the generosity of God. There is room in His heart for all of us. He is constantly offering us His delight, and when we engage it, we become empowered to appreciate one another. While under the influence of comparison, you see friends through a selfish lens—how they limit or diminish who you can be. When you begin to practice gratitude for your life, for God's pleasure and for your friends, you can perceive differences as God intended—as gifts. You're free to ask the Father questions about what you see in your closest friends without shame and then talk to Him about what you notice. Let Him open up your concerns and fill them with His perspective. Are their strengths a picture of what is possible for you? If so, let gratitude for what they bring to the table inspire you to ask them for help. Is it possible that in the chatter of comparison you've stopped hearing what the Father loves about you? Has your obsession with your own enough-ness left you distracted? Where is He longing for you to move into celebration—an appreciation for the richness and depth that diversity adds to your life? A posture of gratitude creates space for friends to add to your life, while comparison suggests they take away from it.

PROMPT: Are your friendships tense with the struggle of comparison? Have your interactions become full of judgment—constant critique of how you measure up? Think of the friendship you feel comparison the strongest in. Ask yourself, *Why am I so uncomfortable with our differences—what do I believe their strengths imply about me? Why do I believe God put this friend in my life?* Slow down and really let yourself answer truthfully.

PRAYER: "Lord, I repent for focusing on what I don't have instead of what I do. Wake me from the spell of comparison, with the truth of your perspective. Fill me with your dream for my life. Open my eyes to your generosity. My value is not dependent on anyone but Jesus. I choose to practice gratitude today. You have blessed me with a friend, and I choose to receive our differences as a gift, not a threat."

ASSUMPTION

as·sump·tion | \ ə-ˈsəm(p)-shən
: an assuming that something is true

Can we talk about the havoc that assumption wreaks on friendship, especially as seasons shift? The longer you have a friend in your life, the easier it is to assume you always know what they are thinking. *Oh, they won't want to do that*, or, *I know exactly what he meant*. This type of "knowing" leads us to assume we always understand what's going on and tells us, "You don't need to ask." Knowing someone in this way actually creates dead ends in friendship because it disregards the need for vulnerable conversations. Without the need to honestly ask questions, clarify expectations and talk through miscommunications, there isn't room for you and your lifelong friends to learn, to grow and to change. What happens when you're wrong about things you assumed so certainly? Assumption leads you to interact with the *idea* of a person instead of the actual person. Have you ever spent hours frustrated over something you never talked to a friend about because you just knew how it would go? Vulnerability keeps your friendship rooted in reality. Knowing a person is not like knowing an answer. It's more of a promise to keep learning them—to keep asking the right questions and being vulnerable with your process while believing the best about them. Vulnerability gives your friends permission to share what's happening in their world, while you own what's happening in yours. Don't assume what worked in the last season will work in your current one. Don't assume you understand new behaviors—*I never hear from her anymore, she must not have time for me*. Let your friends grow. Talk about what is changing. Search out what makes you both feel known in every season. Don't run from your feelings or ignore them. Instead, face them. This person is worth the work of sorting through these challenges. Don't fall back on what you think you know. Fight to keep the gift you've been given. The truth is that the struggle to stay connected—that willingness to be vulnerable in tension—is what produces a secure love, a deep knowing that goes far beyond what assumption would teach you.

PROMPT: Are you hiding behind your assumptions in friendships? Are you afraid to have the kinds of conversations that help redefine expectations in each season? Think of a specific friendship. Ask yourself, *Where is assumption keeping me from really opening up to this friend? Why am I afraid to talk about the tension I feel?* Slow down and really let yourself answer truthfully.

PRAYER: "Lord, forgive me for choosing control over connection. Help me let go of my assumptions and move toward others in vulnerability. Only you know our stories in full. I choose to lean into your understanding, not my own. Show me where my assumptions have clouded my view of my friend. Today, I choose to pursue this friendship with a heart that seeks to understand."

PERFORMANCE

per·for·mance | \ pər-för-mən(t)s
: a public presentation or exhibition
: the action of representing a character in a play

When you love someone, you want to give them your best. But it's easy for that desire to lead to exhausting cycles of performance in friendship. *I'll be what they want, need or expect.* In reality, performance projects the message, "I'm afraid to actually let you love me." It's ridiculous to believe that true friends won't make mistakes, don't set boundaries and can't have needs—but so many of us behave as if these things shouldn't have to be addressed. When we perform for our friends, hoping desperately not to fail them, we rob friendship of the tension that actually builds trust. Real bonding comes from how your friends handle those very things—mistakes, boundaries and needs. Allowing ourselves to be human in our friendships is the only way to form real connection. Say your friend invites you to a party. You feel exhausted but think, *Would she really be okay if I don't go?* So, you go—you perform. Now, some of you might be thinking, *But wait, that's not performing, that's being a good friend.* Is it? By not opening up to your friend and assuming you knew what she wanted, you actually didn't grow in trust with your friend—you grew to trust your perception more. Performance pushes you to evade moments where someone might actually have to practice loving you. What if you talked with your friend and told her you didn't have the capacity to go this time? What if they were disappointed but didn't let that ruin their view of you? Real trust could grow. This works both ways. You don't have to be the friend who always hides disappointment and acts fine. Instead of performing, actually let yourself feel, process with the Father and then in love, talk openly. Performance in friendships will wear you out. It leaves so much room for insecurity. Trust grows when we stop performing and get real about our mistakes, boundaries and needs with the friends we love. Receiving love in the places we were afraid to fail lessens anxiety and heightens confidence.

PROMPT: Do you feel exhausted from trying so hard to please in friendship? Are you anxious, walking around on eggshells, afraid to fail? Stop and ask yourself, *Am I performing for my friends? Am I running from the tension that arises from making mistakes, setting boundaries and vocalizing needs?* Slow down and really let yourself answer truthfully.

PRAYER: "Lord, I repent for hiding my true self behind my performance. Help me let go of the expectation to be perfect. I don't have to be the best. I choose to instead embrace a humble posture that allows friends to extend grace when I cannot meet their wants, needs or expectations. I too will offer my friends permission to be human—to express their struggles and not despise their limitations. Fill my heart with trust as I grow in honesty with my friends."

WINDOWS AND DOORS

writing and photograph by CHRIS MILLER

IF YOU WERE TO STAND IN MY FRONT YARD AND PEER THROUGH THE LARGE, STREET-FACING WINDOWS OF MY HOME DAY AFTER DAY, WOULD YOU SAY THAT YOU KNEW ME?

Would you yourself feel known by me? Through the windows of my home, you might catch glimpses of me and my family that lend to an understanding of who we are and what we value, but it would not mean that you *knew* us—because that occurs inside the home. For this to happen, you would have to stand at the door, knock and possibly be given entry into the intimacy of our lives and our personal residence. Windows merely allow visibility to an environment while doors create access to the inside.

For most of our modern lives, we peer through handheld glass panes that offer us a controlled view into each other's lives and worlds that we hope to be a part of in some small way. The way you represent yourself on social media may give clues to the details of your life, but at best, your friends, family and numerous followers witness a mere window, a glimpse through the glass into the actual reality of your life story. Social media has become the "second space" where you live out portions of your real life: sharing, posting, following, unfollowing, liking, blocking, editing—all in the pursuit of connection. Social networks promise effortless friendship, endless attention and vibrant community but continually reveal the truth that real world connection takes time and work. Social media was not made to foster true human vulnerability. By design, it lacks the intimate risk of sharing face-to-face and therefore cannot actually meet our deep need to be known.

You have a valid human need for connection with God, with others and with your own heart. This is not to your shame, and the sooner you acknowledge it, the quicker you can work to change your habits and create a new normal. The problem is that some of your expectations for connection through social media are most likely unrealistic and impossible to meet. Pete Scazzero says, "Expectations are only valid when they have been mutually agreed upon."[2] This rings true for our lives online. Do you have a baseline to obtain a certain amount of likes on any post you make? Is this reasonable? What if you get no likes? Was it worth posting at all? If you leave a comment on someone's page or post, do you feel entitled to an immediate response? If you don't get the attention you desire, then block a friend and wait for them to notice, are you practicing courage or are you punishing? How are these questions in your "second space" affecting the life you are actually living every day?

I manage several social media accounts for work, ministry and personal use. I love having the ability to visually communicate and share news and information for myself, my family and our community. It feels like opening a window to the world, inviting people to follow our experience. In reality, it is only the tip of the iceberg. There is no way I can actually come close to sharing the total scope of all that we put our hands to each day. I love the medium but feel its real-world limitation. There are moments reserved solely for those who can fit around the dinner table, squeeze into a living room or gather under the rafters of our meeting space. Not every moment is meant to be broadcast! These are treasured times when the record light is off and there is room to simply be. In these times of perpetual sharing, life needs moments where we close the windows, draw the curtains and open the door to the people we are growing in community with, making space and time for deep and meaningful connection.

How many of us perceive the windows of social media as doors—generating assumptions based on the small amount we see? You get to decide how you will engage social media and represent your life, your family and your community online. You have an incredible opportunity to powerfully and thoughtfully open the windows and let the world in. In the same way, you get to choose who you will open your life to and offer a doorway for the people you want to build with.

HOW TO PRACTICE

1. What are my windows?
2. Do I need to close a door?
3. What are my expectations?
4. Replace the screen.
5. Invite the Holy Spirit.

1. WHAT ARE MY WINDOWS?

What are the things in my life I want to open up as windows for others to see? How can I adjust what I share on social media to reflect this?

Examples: "I may share moments from my family, my workplace, my friendships and the things I am creating and growing in," or, "I am going to bravely share a photo or video each week of something I am working on," or, "Instead of only showing the most impressive moments of my life, I am going to actively share a minimum of one moment of gratitude from my workweek, highlighting something normal and ordinary."

2. DO I NEED TO CLOSE A DOOR?

Have I invited others to come into sacred and sensitive parts of my life where they don't belong?

Examples: "I shared difficult and deeply personal news on social media and expected to feel validated," or, "I vented my confused and frustrated feelings without talking to any mentors and close friends in person," or, "I have been hoping that if I keep writing comments on the posts of people I admire, it will cause them to notice me and hopefully give me access to their lives."

3. WHAT ARE MY EXPECTATIONS?

How are my expectations for social media setting me up for disappointment?

Examples: "I've been leaving comments and sending private messages to people I want to get to know in hopes that they will see my effort, and we can become friends. I feel hurt and offended that they've not responded like I hoped they would," or, "I have been sharing my strongest opinions about politics on social media whenever I feel frustrated about current events. I regret some of the things I have said in heated defense and I feel offended by the responses of others. It's not leading to healthy conversations with people I care about. I actually feel more alone and confused."

4. REPLACE THE SCREEN.

How can I pursue people beyond social media?

Example: "Instead of relying on social media for friend interactions, I can engage my God-given creativity to explore ways of connecting through things I love or want to explore. I can try hosting a monthly dinner at my house and invite people in my community and workplace that I'd like to get to know better. Instead of expecting someone to reach out for a coffee date, I will initiate a day-hike on an upcoming weekend and invite some of the people in my community who like to do active things."

5. INVITE THE HOLY SPIRIT.

Holy Spirit, what do you say about me? How can I pursue a new way to think about my life and my need for connection?

Example: "My precious child, I have made you in my image. The passion of your heart and the electricity of your mind are completely of my design. I made you in my delight for the joy of life-long discovery. In fact, I have hidden myself in all of creation for you to find, calling you each morning to open your ears and eyes to the wonder in the everyday. I made you well. Your desire for relationship is deeply rooted in my image. I long for you to embrace your need and bring it to me. Friendship is a gift I freely give. There is nothing you need to prove, because you are already approved by me. The pleasure of your company was purchased on the Cross. My love has already paved the way. Instead of working to prove your worth, let your heart rest in the truth that you are my beloved, and the banner over every second of your life is *love*."

LEAST OF these

by ERIN GRAVITT
artwork by MORGAN CAMPBELL

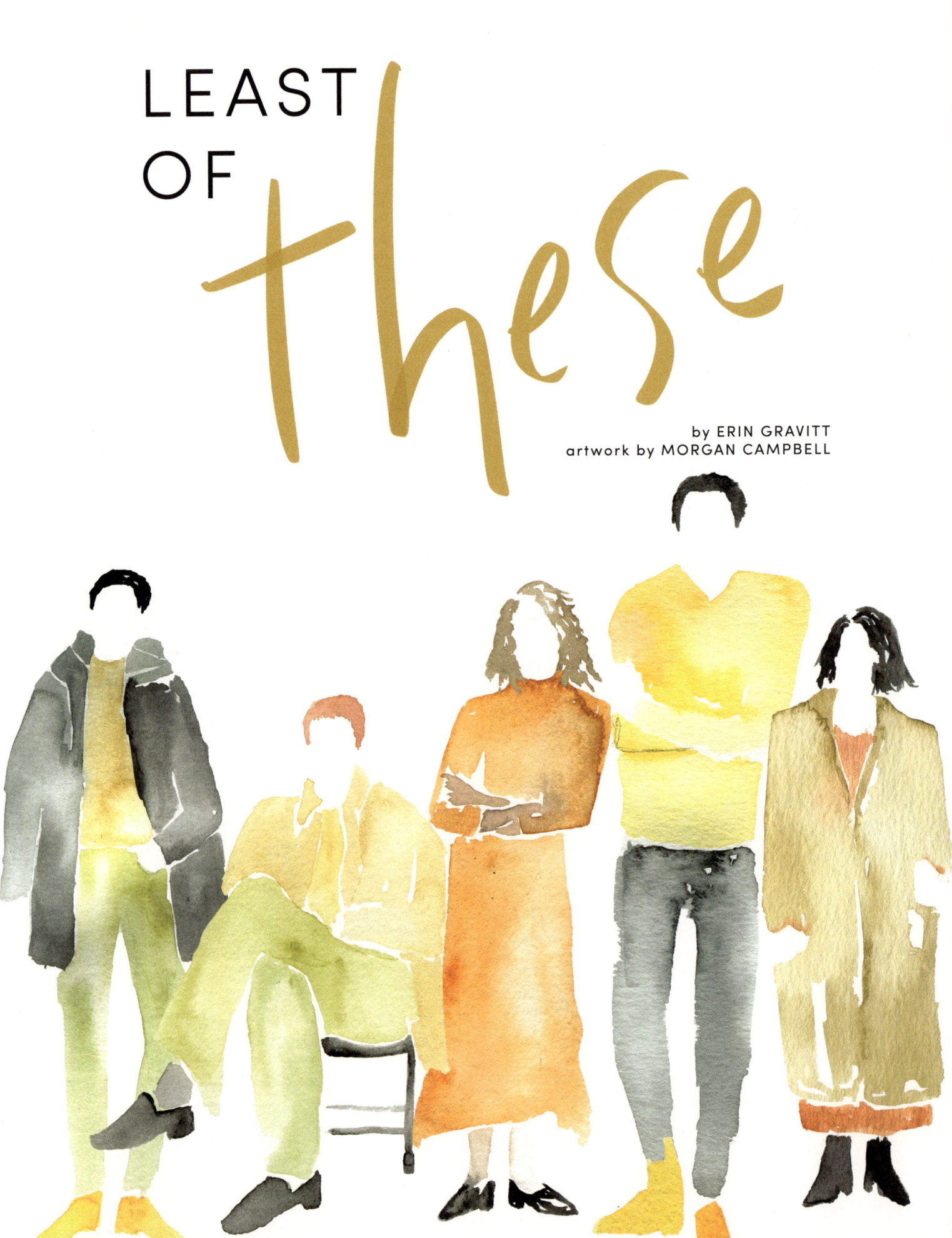

Being a cynic has become a default in our culture. In social media, the government, the news, in our own communities and families, there are a million things to pick apart and judge.

When we see someone else struggling, our responses range from pity to comparison to self-exaltation: *Poor them. What did they do to deserve that? At least I have my life together.* We fall into a ditch of skepticism and negativity. Judging others is quicker and more comfortable than admitting our own struggles and shortcomings. Judgment and pride are always ready to stroke our egos with soothing words that give us a false sense of superiority: *People are crazy. What is wrong with the world?* Scoffing at an easy target—the broken, the poor, the ignorant—deflates our hope and distances us from God's heart.

My first real job was an all-encompassing, immersive dive into social work, a world I knew nothing about. In my role, I managed volunteers, enabling them to compassionately serve men and women in our community who needed help in countless areas of their lives. Every day I encountered broken people, broken relationships, a broken culture. I would see clients who were in total despair, struggling in poverty and cycles of abuse. Some were genuinely seeking help, wanting so badly to change their situation. Others asked for help without following through to make positive change. At first I felt righteous anger toward the pain and darkness of the world. *These men and women are created in God's image! How can I tell them about how much God loves them? How can I bring breakthrough for them?* I thought of myself as a superwoman of light and hope. But after a year of acclimating to the culture shock of my new job, I started to feel drained. I felt fatigued—so many bad things happening to people and so many terrible choices. *Lord, how am I going to help all these people? Will anything I say or do actually make a difference?* And after the weariness came cynicism. My heart hardened. I felt taken advantage of; I started to view my time with clients in a formulaic way: *Let's just get this over with. I could be spending my time doing more important things.*

Repeated failures can make us cynical. When we're met with seemingly hopeless circumstances and people, it's our impulse to try to protect ourselves from disappointment. One way to avoid disappointment is to simply give up hope: *This will never change. Why should I invest in this?* Without fully realizing it, judgment had seeped into my heart, and it became a lens through which I saw everyone. Instead of a paradigm full of hope and possibility rooted in Christ, I gave into cynicism; every scenario felt like defeat, sinking bricks and dead ends. I was forfeiting a life of buoyancy, where the Father invites me to look through His eyes.

I was unaware of how cynical I'd become, but the Lord was determined to protect the softness of my heart. On a normal day at work, our office received a letter in the mail from a supporter of our organization. She shared a simple encouragement and Scripture with our staff that the Lord used to open my eyes: "The King will reply, 'Truly I tell you, whatever you did for one of the least of these brothers and sisters of mine, you did for me'" (Matthew 25:40, NIV). I felt conviction pierce my heart and I began to cry. Sometimes tears are what must come to soften the hardness of cynicism. I heard the Lord's kindness as He said to my spirit, "Erin, don't you see me in them? And don't you see yourself? You're no different than them; you need help just as they need help." I repented and made an exchange with Jesus that day, my judgment and hopelessness for His compassion and hope. I opened my heart to receiving the way He sees people, always worthy of value and investment.

There's no easy way to love the broken; I can't give you a play-by-play on how to do it perfectly. But this was a turning point for me. Here are two things the Lord invited me to start practicing:

1. IMAGINE WITH GOD'S VISION.

In my mind, our clients had lost their humanity, but really, I had lost vision. This Scripture helped me visualize people differently, through the heart of Jesus. Everyday I began to meditate on Matthew 25:40 and actively imagine clients as Jesus as they walked through the doors of my office. This opened my heart to God's hope instead of my limited viewpoint.

2. PRACTICE "I NEED HELP, TOO."

You can't impact something you're not willing to love. Many of us want to be helpers, but we must first be helped by the Lord. I let Him pierce my heart, surrendering my arrogance to His healing and love. This is the beauty of being connected in empathy to our culture and the world. We all need help, and we can actually make a profound difference when we see ourselves in others' brokenness. May we all reject cynicism, that suspicion that cripples and tangles the soul, and instead, love humanity.

PROMPT: Where are judgment and cynicism your default patterns? Think about the people in your culture and everyday life who may get on your nerves. Maybe it's the homeless person you drive by once a week asking for help at the traffic intersection; the harried mom at the store trying to appease her screaming kid; a customer service rep on the other end of the phone who has put you on hold once again. Instead of hurling judgment at them in your heart, practice coming into agreement with God's vision. Pick one of these people you've recently encountered, and imagine Jesus in their place. How might your perspective change if Jesus was on the other end of the customer service line or in the grocery store? Let Jesus challenge you and grow your compassion.

OPENING up in VULNERABILITY

TWO WAY STREET

Writing and photograph by
MORGAN CAMPBELL

True friendship is a two-way street.

It requires the participation of two people, both opening up—giving access to their thoughts and feelings.

For years, I was unaware of how imbalanced my approach to connection was. I was a one-way street: the one everyone could rely on, who never needed anything in return. I was the friend who always listened. I made space for my friends to talk about things they were going through. I asked questions and gave advice, but quickly glazed over any questions that required true vulnerability on my end. I would fill my friends in on what my daily life looked like, but never thought about sharing my feelings or how I was being affected. I thought I was being vulnerable until I started noticing how alone and confused I felt. *Why aren't my friends asking me more questions? Does anyone really know me?* The gears were grinding, and I could feel my capacity for others wearing down under my own tension. I was giving everything I had to everyone else, but I wasn't allowing anyone to invest in me.

It wasn't until one night at my small group that I realized how lost I was. The whole night was about vulnerability. We were each asked to open up and share our story with the group. Seven minutes of non-stop sharing—my nightmare come to life. *How is this going to go? What is everyone going to think? I have no idea how to do this*, I thought. I braced myself and tried to plow through it, but right in the middle of sharing I got emotional. I wasn't even sure why. Everyone could feel the tension of my process and the pain I was carrying. For the first time, I was telling someone else something about *me*. I was getting vulnerable.

To my surprise, I was met with understanding. One friend in particular offered me a picture that helped me understand how I was feeling. He compared me to a character from a Dr. Seuss book, Thidwick the big-hearted moose. As he started describing Thidwick—a moose with big antlers who was unable to move forward from the weight of all the forest animals he had allowed to nest in them—it was like a light bulb went off. *THAT'S ME!* I felt unable to move forward, imbalanced and frustrated. I felt responsible to carry my friends. Always accommodating, never asking for anything in return. The Father used that picture to ask me a question, "What would happen if you let go of the pressure to always carry others and started letting others also carry you?"

We teach our friends how to treat us. A lack of vulnerability sends the message, *I have it all together; I don't need your help.* If you want to bring balance to your relationships, you have to look at your patterns of relating and take ownership for how your behavior has affected things. It's not your friends' job to hunt down the truth of what's happening in your inner world. Once I saw how little access I was giving my friends to my heart, I began to ask the Lord for ways I could start to open up and send a new message, *I want you to know things about me. I need you in my life.* I started small. I practiced reaching out. When I was having a hard time, instead of waiting for my friends to notice, I would take a deep breath, invite the Holy Spirit to help me and say something like, "I'm having a tough time and I would love some help talking it through. Would you be open to that?" I didn't know what to expect. I was afraid my friends would be overwhelmed but I was met with empathetic responses. I found that I had a need to externalize my thoughts, and often that was the starting place for building connection. They wanted to support me, but I had to give them the opportunity.

I remember a moment when I knew things were different. It had been a hard day. Tears welled up in my eyes as my roommate walked through the door. All my old instincts told me to run away and find an isolated spot to cry, but I felt the Holy Spirit's familiar whisper: "Stay. Open up." I chose to let one of my best friends see my honest tears. She sat with me. She listened and empathized. It left me feeling liberated and connected. For months I had been building a road for her to be able to reach me. I had taught her, *I love your company and wisdom. You're welcome here.* I felt the gift of relief wash over me as I let myself be carried. Vulnerability and trust were flowing both ways. This friendship had become a two-way street and I felt known.

REFLECT: What messages are you sending your friends? Does your behavior line up with what you actually want in friendship?

PROMPT: Ask the Lord, "Where am I hiding from my friends?" Journal His response.

PRACTICE: Initiate a friend this week about a part of your heart you want to share. When I first practiced asking for help, I admitted what I needed but gave my friend space to answer, "I'm having a tough time and I would love some help talking it through. Would you be open to that?" Be brave and take the risk of opening up!

GIVING IN TO TEAM

by JAKE STEVENS   /   photograph by JONO MACSORLEY

I love being on a team. I love problem-solving, asking questions and figuring out the best way to execute a plan. At A Place for the Heart, I'm part of a few different departments and in each I've had to learn how to fight for our common goal and abandon my own independent instincts.

I've learned that my teammates can become one of two things: obstacles in the way or partners who can help shoulder the weight that I can't carry on my own. I've had to lay down my ideas of what is best in order to grow into my role and serve my team. These are a few things I've learned along the way that have transformed my perspective.

The way I behave affects my teammates, whether I like it or not. I used to assume that my behavior didn't affect anyone else. I'd bring my own problems into meetings with me: *I've had a tough day—that dumb lawn mower broke down again.* I was so busy with my thoughts, searching for solutions to my own problems, that I wouldn't bring any productive ideas to the table. I viewed my team as another thing on my overwhelming to-do list. Whenever meetings seemed to take too long, I was annoyed. *I have a hundred other things I could be doing right now.* In my frustration, I'd get short with people and argumentative. After years of this tendency, no one on my team knew which Jake to expect. On a good day, I was friendly, helpful and motivated. On a bad day, I was charged, sarcastic and anxious to wrap up the meeting. My friends felt confused. On those bad days, I'd watch many of them either shut down or fight back. Bottom line: my inconsistency was breaking trust. It was throwing a proverbial wrench into the gears.

I didn't know it then, but really all I wanted was to feel in control of my day. I didn't want to share space with my teammates because they would slow me down, or worse, they might discover I was inadequate. *Do I have what it takes to be here? It's better if I work alone; what I have to contribute isn't even wanted.* I was showing up to meetings ready to cope at every turn, and everyone could see it. That's the vulnerability of being on a team; you cannot hide very long.

The honest truth is that my behavior was pointing to a bigger fear: the fear that I'm incapable. Incapable of work relationships. Incapable of being on a team. Incapable of doing a good job. This fear has to be dealt with one way or the other. I can either do the work to resolve it or I can cope with it. Resolving it means I let it affect me in a way that is often uncomfortable. I take it to the Lord, work it out and it is exchanged there: between Father and child. Coping means I avoid letting it affect me. I ignore my emotions and eventually my pain leaks out onto the team around me: through my sharp tone, my disagreement, my bad attitude. This is the selfish way. Sacrificing other people's trust for my own comfort.

I'll never forget the first time I realized how selfish and heart-breaking my approach was. I was sitting with a counselor I admired and respected; a guy who had gone through the kind of pain I encountered in my own story. "You need to let the people you work with every day really tell you how you're affecting them, otherwise you really have no reason to change." A scary prompt, but wild enough to work. I need to know how other people experience me, and it's not realistic to assume I know the way that I'm affecting them. Asking open-handedly for someone's honest thoughts helps bring awareness, and it brought forth my own transformation. Receiving honest feedback can hurt, but it is a key to creating a healthy, thriving team.

Another part of my breakthrough has been actively pursuing a blame-free mindset. Before I go into a meeting, I remind myself that I'm accountable for my actions. When I realize I'm getting really negative, I practice honesty with myself: *No one in this room caused my bad mood. There is no one to blame.* Then I ask, *What do I need right now? Do I need to let my team know that I had a hard day?* If I do, I practice honesty with my team, "I wanted to let you guys know from the top that I'm having a hard day. I'm not upset with any of you. I just want to be honest and let you know that I'm struggling." I've got pretty amazing teammates. Doing this not only helps them, but it also helps me. They'll often follow-up with asking if I need anything, and I do my best to answer honestly. Vocalizing that I'm struggling immediately shuts down the feeling of being alone and out of control. When I speak up, I close the mouth of the enemy.

Another step I've taken in engaging my team is coming in more prepared. Before going into a meeting or communicating with someone on my team, I take a minute and I resolve to stay clear and centered. *I get to decide how I enter this meeting, I am a valuable part of this team, so I am going to show up in my mind and heart.* I set my disposition before I engage others. This helps me connect to the truth that I am powerful. An African Proverb says, "If you want to go fast, go alone but if you want to go far, go together," and this sums up so much of what I've learned in the past decade of working in a team.

PROMPT: Think about how you relate to your team. Are you passive, disappearing in the group, unable to speak up when you have ideas? Are you moody, present one day and preoccupied the next? Are you defensive and difficult to work with? Write down a few thoughts in your journal. What fear may be beneath your behavior? Ask the Holy Spirit for insight. Try to think of a specific scenario where your negative behavior was present in a team setting and complete an Honesty Tool (see pg. 42).

PRACTICE: Ask someone how you are affecting them or the team. Give them space to respond; they may need some time to think about it. Be patient and remember that feedback creates a pathway of transformation.

by JD GRAVITT

Passivity is like being dunked in an ice bath— you gasp for air as the frozen shock hits your senses. You feel numb, as though all strength has left your body and paralysis sinks into your limbs. You feel like a black and white sketch in a world of color, so fragile that a slight breeze might knock you over.

The first time I felt the frigid, breath-taking presence of this silent anxiety, I was six. In my hand I held a note from my teacher, "Applies himself well in class, but I can't get him to sit still. Talks out of turn." It wasn't the first time I got a note like this. The weight of the accumulating negative responses from my teacher was enough to set into motion the understanding that I was bad, defective, imperfect. I didn't realize it then, but at the age of six, I was already learning to give up, to stay quiet, to play the victim.

Throughout my life, I've processed many of my failures through that same filter, *What's the point? My opinion doesn't matter.* It would come up suddenly in all kinds of situations—at work, with my boss, in a pretty normal moment with friends—and all of a sudden, I'd feel like that same little boy, hanging his head low.

Passivity has become my attempt to protect that little boy. It's a strategy I've carried into my adulthood to handle stress, the demands of life and the things I'm afraid of. When I choose passivity, it looks like inaction. It happens in a variety of ways: When I ignore that something's off with a friend. When making simple decisions takes way too long. When someone argues a loud opinion at the dinner table, and I internally retreat deep within my skin and bones for fear that my voice is no match for theirs. In all of these moments, I'm believing there's a threat that doesn't actually exist. As if life is fragile, and making one mistake will have irreparable consequences. So the safest option is to do nothing at all.

Passivity is not what it seems. We like to relate it to peace and calmness. It's not that. Passivity appears harmless—a quieter personality option, one that errs on the side of niceness. But the kind of passivity I'm talking about is inaction rooted in fear. And the truth is, it's detrimental to everything meaningful in our lives. Passivity literally means, "acceptance of what happens, without active response or resistance," according to the New Oxford American dictionary.[3] It offers the deception of safety through the acceptance of what happens. It falsely promises that everything will work out if you just leave the situation alone.

In actuality, passivity costs everything. It takes your voice, your opinion and your desires. Passivity is like a rust that seizes mobility and deteriorates your value. It robs dreams and silences possibility. Passivity will lead us to forfeit things that already belong to us. For fear of rejection, we hesitate with friends who already love us. We waste time doubting our acceptance instead of stepping up in our authority as sons and daughters. We move backwards, putting on fig leaves over our royal robes.

I must confess that I somehow think I am more holy or "Christ-like" when I passively avoid conflict and disagreements. So many of us have come to believe that a lack of conflict or adversity is more representative of Jesus' Kingdom culture. It's not. Life is rarely smooth sailing; we are in a war and things will go wrong. There is never a moment when being passive will help someone you love or strengthen your relationship with Jesus. As a man and as a son of God, I am made for action and born to be powerful. Jesus was constantly moving against the injustice He saw in the world. He disrupted funerals and flipped tables in church. He wasn't passive. He resisted the kingdom of this world to bring His Kingdom. He knew that His presence mattered, that He was born with purpose. We must learn to hate the lies that bind us in passivity and blatantly contradict every truth and promise we have in Jesus.

When we let Jesus tell us who we are, it allows us to step beyond passivity and into action. We stop being passive, not because we're trying harder but because we're believing better. We are believing that we are chosen, that we are a royal priesthood, that we are the beloved of the Father. And when we step into our true identity as sons and daughters, we will behave accordingly. We will boldly show up in our lives, exercising the freedom to be our true selves.

If you find yourself at war with passivity, there are many options to take back ground.

Take Inventory

Admit to yourself how you are feeling. Ask yourself a few questions: *Do I feel paralyzed? Do I feel tension in my body? Am I afraid of making a wrong decision?* All of these are good indicators that passivity is present. Ask yourself, *What is the source of the passivity?* Is there a specific fear or belief that is motivating you to be passive? What is the worst that you believe will happen? Take a breath and take heart! Awareness is the first key to victory. Finding and articulating what's happening will help you gain traction in the thick of passivity.

Take Back Your Voice

Once you are aware of what's going on, activate your voice. Passivity thrives in silence, so it's important that you speak out loud. Find a quiet place to tell God what you are feeling. Describe how you're seeing yourself to Him. In contrast, ask Him how He sees you. Let Him show you your true self and speak courage to your identity. Then share honestly with a close friend—own the lie you've believed and the truth you're fighting for. Be courageous and invite them into agreement for the battle you want to win. By sharing with a friend, you receive the gift of unity and the power of agreement.

Take a Risk

Passivity thrives in hesitation and indecision. Sometimes we just need to take action. In moments of passivity, making a decision, even if it's imperfect, is better than staying indecisive. Mistakes are not the enemy. A wrong choice can turn into a stepping stone for a future victory. So finding and choosing a course of action will create the energy and momentum you need to press through passivity.

Passivity is always an option for coping with life and sometimes you are going to find yourself in the familiar numbness of being passive. That's okay. The point isn't that passivity would stop becoming an option. The point is that you would recognize it when it comes, and have the courage to choose the truth: You are powerful. I charge you to stay aware and be vigilant. Practicing awareness in everyday moments stops the spread of passivity and allows you to take ground. The small victories that you win each day add up to a life of freedom. Be patient with yourself and let the Lord reintroduce you to the truth of your identity.

THE NEW GUY

by ZAC VANCE
artwork by MORGAN CAMPBELL

AT THE START OF MY ADULT CAREER, I WAS THE NEW GUY BECOMING A PART OF A COMMUNITY OF BELIEVERS THAT WAS ESTABLISHED AND THRIVING. IMMEDIATELY I NOTICED THAT FRIENDSHIP AND CONNECTION WERE HARD FOR ME. FOR THE FIRST TIME IN A LONG TIME, I WAS THE ODD MAN OUT.

I perceived this community to have no need for me and I struggled to feel valuable when everyone was clearly operating just fine without me. My inner dialogue was incessant, *You need to catch up. Become important. Make yourself needed.* These thoughts were sabotaging my genuine enjoyment of the people around me, enslaving me to an idea of who I thought I should be. Others pursued me by asking about my work, and I treated our interactions as a chance to rack up more "points." When it became my turn to listen, I didn't give them my full attention. Rather, I was preoccupied with the best way to tailor my responses to that individual so that they would like me or find my presence useful. I didn't mean to be self-focused, but my insecurities were flaring and I didn't know how to relate to my new community when I didn't feel important. In a matter of months I was exhausted and unhappy amongst some of the strongest, most joyful believers I had ever been around. I wasn't sure what to do, but I knew I needed a change.

In my frustration, I cried out to the Lord. "God, why is relating to this community so hard?" He gently broke down my walls to show me the heart of my insecurity—that at the core of my interactions, I didn't believe that I was enough. I had spent years building up a personal resumé in my mind, becoming the judge of my own worthiness, leaving little room for grace. God knew I needed a perspective shift and gave me the gift of saying once again, "Zac, you are enough. You are a good gift. You are my unique breath never to be repeated." God brought me back to the teachings from Dietrich Bonhoeffer, specifically this passage: "The person who loves their dream of community will destroy community, but the person who loves those around them will create community."4 I had a dream of community where first and foremost I would be needed, and it was destroying me. I wanted to perform for my place amongst these believers. Dinners, conversations, cleaning up, even worship had become about feeling the room so I could secure my part in it. I had stopped being able to see others and only perceived how they saw me. I chose to perform in community and I failed to simply love those around me, chiefly myself.

The shift was subtle from the outside and earth shattering in my inner world. Hearing and believing that I am a beloved son of my Father as I entered back into community gave me confidence to be myself. This new belief created space to truly see and hear the hearts of those around me. A talk over coffee was no longer a tenuous game of balance, but a place to know and be known. I left these conversations feeling pursued in friendship, enjoying others rather than judging myself. While many of my outward actions remained the same, my inward motivations were creating life in and around me.

God used this integration into a new community to challenge what I truly believed about myself. Where I wanted to prove my value to a community, God wanted to reveal that my value was never in question. I am simply valuable because He says so. Now, I enjoy myself within community more than I ever have and the love that I have for those around me is authentic and life-giving.

PROMPT: Where is a place where you feel distracted or insecure within your community? In your journal, jot down a relationship or scenario where this insecurity surfaces the most. Invite the Holy Spirit to show you what you are actually believing to be true about yourself in this moment. In faith, ask Him what He believes about you instead. Journal His voice, and let confidence in your identity in Him wash over you.

It was a familiar spot: hiding in the bathroom by myself, door closed, lost under the weight of sadness. It was Mother's Day. I tried to avoid social media, knowing that every sweet photo of a friend smiling with their mother would sting; every appreciative caption a reminder of my loss. I tried to prepare my heart. I knew it was coming, and I knew it would be painful, just like the three Mother's Days before it. Just like the three anniversaries of her passing. Just like the four Thanksgivings and Christmases that missed her presence. I had braced myself as best as I knew how, but I was still on the floor. Still breathless from sorrow. Still wishing she was here so I could post my own happy photo and call her to brighten up her day.

    Grief is mysterious. I think Antoine de Saint-Exupéry said it best: "It is such a mysterious place, the land of tears."[5] I am seven years into navigating grief's terrain. I am young, and yet already a quarter of my life has been spent trying to learn the lay of this land. It's often felt like wandering the desert: Empty. Endless. Unbearably uncomfortable. Other times it's felt like being stranded at sea: Tumultuous. Overpowering. Terrifying. For many years, the only consistent thing I felt in my grief was loneliness.

GRIEF'S TERRAIN

by ALLIE SAMPSON | photography by MORGAN CAMPBELL

I spent the first year after losing my mom punishing God with my silence and separation. Trust had been broken, and I wasn't eager to rebuild. I felt betrayed. I put distance between us and made a point to move away when I felt Him getting close. But even with all my distance, He consistently came. I was moved by His loyalty. He wasn't offended by my anger or repelled by my tangled mess of emotions. Even more surprising was His patience. He didn't pressure me to be okay or demand that I profess His goodness in the middle of my crisis. He won my heart slowly through His consistency—sitting beside me in my sadness with no agenda to fix my pain and no hurried posture toward my healing. He knew I needed Him to be patient, and He honored it.

I won't forget it. Jesus came like He always does and sat with me on the floor. My heavy heart with a full-weighted lean against His shoulder. He offered His familiar comfort and expressed appreciation that I'd let Him come close again. I felt His reassurance that my pain was not too much, and that the lost feelings did not mean I was out of His reach. Gently, He offered me a choice: "Allie, you could stay in this place alone. Or you could invite a friend to come here with you." I recoiled at the thought.

My entire life, I have taken it upon myself to process challenge and difficulty alone. Perhaps it is my only child-ness, or my need to prove that I am capable. Maybe it's my desire to ease the burden of those around me, or the belief that needy people eventually get left alone in the end. Whatever perfect storm led me to this moment, I was on the floor, reluctant to leave. Letting the Lord sit with me in my suffering had taken significant work. Buying in to the truth that He never approaches me with the motivation of fixing me was a hard-won victory. I didn't trust other people to approach me with the same sensitivity—not even my closest and safest friends.

I sat and argued with Jesus. He challenged me, and I struggled to rise to the occasion. "Allie, I will always meet you in your suffering, but it is important to me that you know you're not alone. Let me come to you through a friend. Will you make space for me to meet you like this?" "No." Silence slipped between us. A capsized, "I'm sorry, God," fell from my discouraged heart.

I want to be clear. It wasn't that I wanted to stay leaned up against the bathtub alone. I was desperate to feel known in the places of my deepest suffering. I craved connection—a companion in the desert who could point me to water; a friend on the boat who could identify a shoreline in the midst of the storm. But accessing that kind of connection felt incredibly risky. That kind of vulnerability—perhaps, the only true kind—required me to reach beyond fear. Not just beyond the surface-level insecurities: *She'll think I'm weird. This is so awkward.* But the ones that lurked in the deepest deep: *The quickest way to lose friends is to ask too much of them; you're leeching the life out of her with your problems. Kind friends don't drag others into the desert with them. The key to keeping friends is keeping them happy. If you were a real Christian, Jesus would be enough for you and all of your problems.*

I wanted off the floor, but getting up required deeper surrender, and another willingness to let go. A willingness to let go of the *What ifs* and *You can'ts* I had agreed with for three grief-stricken years. It required a willingness to be wrong about my friends and the assumptions I'd made about their capacities for my needs. And deeper still, it required a willingness to be wrong about the Lord yet again: God wasn't trying to make me so dependent on Him that I would never need another meaningful human relationship. That's what I believed. But here He was, offering me a direct invitation into the opposite. "Allie, your friend is in the next room, you could tell her what's going on. She'd really love to support you."

The problem in arguing with God is that He is quite persuasive. For a girl who likes to win, I've had to learn the art of losing to Him. Surrender is the meeting place of relief. I wrestled, I weighed, I waited. And then, locking eyes with Jesus I said, "Okay, I'm willing."

The events that followed weren't particularly profound or spiritual. I got off the floor and found my friend in the next room, just like Jesus said I would. I opened up about how hard the day was and simply confessed, "I really miss my mom today." My friend made a spot for me beside her and said, "I've been thinking about you all day. I'm so sorry today's so painful for you." And then she let me cry. Arm wrapped around me in familiar comfort. Silence slipping between us. Sitting with me in my sadness, with no agenda to fix my pain and no hurried posture toward my healing. Relief. And her expressed appreciation for the opportunity to come close. Just like Jesus.

This is only one instance in a seven-year series of instances. I have been practicing vulnerability with my dearest friends over and over. Opening up my grief still requires me to make a powerful choice, but the beauty is that I now experience far more than loneliness in my sorrow. What started as silent isolation in the bathroom has grown into powerful, proactive communication. The choice to reach out to friends on hard anniversaries and holidays. Checking in with my heart, asking myself, *How am I really doing? Do I need anything?* In my need to grieve, I have found that processing sorrow with friends has drastically reduced the amount of time I spend feeling lost. Ten minutes of courage and candor brings resolve that used to take weeks of wandering to find.

There are still many days when I feel the temptation to stay sad alone. I still experience the lost feelings. Still have days that sweep me back out to sea or drop me in the middle of the desert. These days will continue to come for the rest of my life. But the difference is that when they do, I am reminded of Jesus' arm around me and His kind challenge to stand up. I was not created to hide my sorrow and manage it alone. I was created for connection, made to be met in joy *and* in suffering.

PROMPT: Have you isolated yourself in your sorrow? Have you avoided sharing the weight of your emotions with the Lord and with your friends out of fear that they will not be willing to support you? Reflect honestly on these questions, and journal a simple prayer of repentance. Let Him speak back to you.

PRACTICE: Invite Jesus into your pain. Ask Him to come meet you in your sorrow. Practice sharing the weight of your suffering with Him. Then ask the Father to highlight a specific friend who is safe to share with. When He has highlighted someone, ask them if you can share honestly about how you're feeling. Share with them what the Lord is speaking to you and any specific days that you anticipate being difficult.

> *"Being deeply moved with tender compassion, Jesus reached out..."* Mark 1:41, TPT

UNDER NEW MANAGEMENT

by JOEL CASE

I used to live under a lot of pressure following Jesus. When it came to sharing my faith or praying for someone, I felt paralyzed by the fear of missing the perfect moment, weighed down with a heavy sense of responsibility for someone else's salvation or breakthrough. *It's all up to me.* I was either fulfilling God's plans or ruining them, and the anxiety of bouncing between the two was unbearable. Time and time again in Scripture, we see Jesus being led by compassion, not anxiety, when it came to reaching out and helping people. Compassion overflows from hearts that know they are beloved. I needed a deeper revelation of His love for me before I could genuinely give it to others.

My intentions started in something real. I loved God from a young age and so badly wanted to be close to Him, but I didn't really know how He felt about me. It seemed safest to assume the worst—that he was angry or disappointed—and perform accordingly. As a teenager, my great desire to please God mixed with my huge imagination to form endless intimidating possibilities. *I should stand up in my school bus and preach the Gospel. I should pray for the blind girl at school to be healed.* Once an idea like this got in my head, it felt impossible to think about anything else. My thoughts taunted me: *Do it! If God is really in you then why can't you just be brave?* God's actual voice felt very far from me in those moments. If I was unable to muster the courage to do what I thought He was saying to do, the whole next week could be spent playing the "What if" game—*What if everyone had gotten saved? What if God really did heal her? How dare I keep that from her.* I would punish myself and repeatedly apologize to God, promising I'd be braver next time. Opportunities to sincerely love people and have fun with God felt like chances to miss Him and fail to measure up yet again. In this way, my reaching out was very self-centered. I spent years of my life haunted by what I hadn't done for God.

By my early twenties, I was drowning under the pressure of perfect performance. My longing to breathe freely and my need to feel loved overwhelmed my fear. *This can't be the way it's supposed to feel.* I asked a friend for help. We prayed together, and it was like my friend's prayers reached in and pulled me up for air. I had a genuine encounter with Jesus that day. I felt the pressure drain from my lungs as I breathed in His joy and delight over me. I started laughing and could hardly stop. I'd been so blind, fumbling through following His will. Now my heart was illuminated with His desire for me. My whole way of thinking—my perception of His character—began to be rewired. It was as if God hung a sign on the door of my mind that said, "Under New Management." I no longer needed to do what anxiety dictated. Instead I was becoming a man led by peace and fueled by compassion.

When thoughts would come that were full of confusion and pressure, I felt God's re-alignment, "That's not how I do business. Let it go." When thoughts came with tenderness and love, I felt bold in His invitation, "Yes, this is how we approach people." My self-centered approach was being replaced with a compassion-centered one. God's thoughts reflect His true nature and the fruit of the Spirit (see Galatians 5:22). His faithfulness always comes through. He orchestrates everything for the good of those who love Him. As I experienced His affection for me, patterns of self-punishment were reshaped by how He loved me—with patience, kindness, gentleness and joy. I was what I'd always longed to be: a beloved son.

I remember one of the first times I tasted the fruit of being filled with God's delight before boldly reaching out to someone else. I noticed a woman who had fallen down a step and injured her knee. Others were around, but no one seemed to be moving towards her. A clear faith rose up in me and I felt the invitation to engage her in her need. I didn't overthink it, I kindly asked her, "Can I pray for you?" "Yes, please," she said with pain and disappointment in her voice. My heart filled with compassion as I sensed that this injury felt like another setback in her life. I knew God wanted to break the cycle of discouragement. I put my hand on her knee and began to pray. I kid you not, before I even got through saying, "In the name of Jesus, be healed," I physically felt her muscle shift under my hand! I finished my prayer just in case—*Could it really have been that simple?* Once I said amen, she got up totally pain free, and without hesitation, walked right out of the building. I felt full of confidence and gratitude. No pressure. Powerful courage. Love from overflow.

When an opportunity to reach out to someone arises, I've learned to ask myself these questions: *Am I connected to the nature of the Father? Am I feeling responsible for this person's healing or salvation? Am I walking on the tightrope of performance, or am I hand in hand with God?*

These questions help slow my mind, and the answers empower me to make decisions rooted in love instead of fear. I still have moments of anxiety, but I have made a practice of turning my thoughts to a Father who leads by joy, not by pressure. If I think I missed a moment, I press into trusting God with that person's story. He is the true hero, not me. Choosing to turn to Him instead of anxiety reminds me that I am loved and have permission to practice and learn.

PROMPT: What are the main "voices" that drive your thoughts and actions? Do you struggle to hear the Father's heart above the noise of anxiety, hopelessness, fear or pressure? What would it look like to come under New Management?

PRACTICE: Write out three recurring thoughts that don't line up with God's nature. Ask the Father for three new thoughts to practice thinking instead. Invite Jesus to be your leader, voicing your desire for Him to rule in your inner world.

TOOL № 1 : THE HONESTY TOOL

let's get honest,

IN VOLUME V: *THE ART OF CONNECTION*, JONATHAN AND MELISSA INTRODUCED THE HONESTY TOOL—A PRACTICAL TOOL USED BY OUR COMMUNITY, DESIGNED TO HELP YOU PROCESS YOUR LIFE WITH THE LORD AND GIVE UNDERSTANDING TO WHAT'S REALLY GOING ON IN MOMENTS OF TENSION. TODAY, WE WANT TO REINTRODUCE YOU TO USING THIS TOOL IN THE VARIOUS RELATIONSHIPS IN YOUR LIFE.

It is impossible to progress in connection without working through some level of conflict. Our community has experienced this truth in many types of relationships: co-workers, roommates, close friends, people we are managing and leading. If there isn't a willingness to confront, to speak respectfully and honestly, then there isn't much room to grow with each other or build trust.

This tool exists to help you care for your heart, and in turn, it will help you care for the hearts of others. All of us want good friendships; we all want to do it right and avoid pain. The unfortunate part of these desires is that sometimes they lead us into suppressing how we really feel, denying our emotions to make others happy. Eventually, this practice will hurt us more than help us. We can end up avoiding a friend because they've hurt us or exploding on a friend and hurting them. Connecting to our hearts and processing tension with the Lord is a vital part of being a good friend.

In the following pages, members from our community open up their honest process in moments of real life tension. It is our desire that you feel empowered and challenged to press into resolve with your heart and with the Father. May you feel inspired to try a new way in your relationships and experience breakthrough.

1 STOP AND ASK

Pray, "Holy Spirit, I need your help. What is really going on?"

To stop and ask for help is to invite the Holy Spirit and His perspective. Inviting His presence into your process is one of the most powerful practices. He has every solution and is fully committed to you. He is the Spirit of Truth and is ready to empower your new process.

"Help me, Lord my God; save me according to your unfailing love."
Psalms 109:26, NIV

GET HONEST

Get your journal and pen and go sit somewhere quiet. Take the risk to write your most honest prayer.

Include your thoughts, emotions and behavior in the situation. This action is humbly admitting that you need help from the One who knows you best. David consistently practiced brutal honesty and neediness for the Father throughout the Psalms. He had a confidence that God wasn't afraid of his humanity, which produced an intimacy that still ministers to our hearts today.

"Search me, God, and know my heart; test me and know my anxious thoughts."
Psalms 139:23, NIV

REFLECT AND EXCHANGE

After completing your most honest prayer, take a moment to read what you wrote and reflect.

Ask yourself, *Are these thoughts true? Am I believing any lies about myself, another person or God?* Underline and create a list of the thoughts and lies you want to exchange for the truth.

Then, pray out loud. Own where you've believed lies and ask God to forgive you. Invite Him to exchange lies for truth.

We cannot give away what we do not own. Learning to own your honest beliefs is the beginning of transformation. It allows us to enter into an exchange with the Father where He replaces lies with truth. You can simply pray, "God I come to you and own that I've believed…(name the lies) and I ask you to forgive me and make an exchange."

"…we take captive every thought to make it obedient to Christ."
II Corinthians 10:5, NIV

LISTEN

Pray, "Holy Spirit, speak to me the truth." Journal His response.

Give Him permission to speak into the vulnerable places in your heart. It is vital that you land this practice in the Father's voice. This tool isn't for self-help, it is meant to cultivate dependency on the Trinity. Always practice landing in His opinion. If the voice of the Lord created the heavens and the earth, He can recreate your inner world. This step requires faith and risk and is always worth it! An indicator that you are on the right track is if you feel seen by the Lord and His nature fills your heart—joy, compassion, peace, love.

"Then you will know the truth, and the truth will set you free." John 8:32, NIV

TOOL №1 : THE HONESTY TOOL

here's my example,

by PHYLLIS UNKEFER

I have a close friend who lives far from me. The day we went from being roommates to living on opposite ends of the country felt like a change in the weather. A cold wind in the middle of summer. We'd seen each other every day for five years—talking, laughing, riding side by side on city buses and confiding in each other with ease. When we both moved away, we felt the sudden distance. Distance goes against everything friendship wants: time together, closeness, the ability to lean against each other when you're both laughing way too hard. Despite living apart, she and I have stayed close. We've flown cross-country to make visits and we've kept talking for years—phone calls, FaceTime, texts. But one year, things got much quieter. Months passed without a word in either direction. I noticed. I wondered why. I started reaching out to her, calling more, sending messages every few weeks. That year, it seemed like most of the effort to initiate connection was coming from my end. It kicked up this feeling of uncertainty. All these questions slipped through my mind, and I was surprised by how sensitive I felt. To the point that I knew I needed to sit down with Jesus and ask for His help.

1

STOP AND ASK

Holy Spirit, why do I feel this way? Would you show me what's happening in my heart?

2 GET HONEST

Lord, I feel like I'm doing all the initiating these days. Why? Is she withdrawing from me? Am I too much? Does she still want this friendship? I'm afraid that I've been replaced by other people in her life. And that's painful. I might not be useful to her anymore. Is it because she doesn't have capacity right now, or does she just not care? Maybe I've been too messy or too selfish or too hard to be with. Did she regret coming to visit me for my birthday? I'm annoyed at how unsure I feel. I keep wanting to pull away from her to protect myself. Or to, just out of the blue, send a ridiculous text like, "Do you hate me now?!" God, I feel rejected. Why don't I feel like you're protecting my heart?

3 REFLECT AND EXCHANGE

I'm too much. I am replaced. Friendships end when I'm no longer useful. Friendship is dangerous. God isn't protecting me. God rejects me.

4 LISTEN

Phyllis, you are deeply loved. You're not too much. I'm changing the channel in your mind so you can hear my affirmation. And I'm removing shame. I'm so fond of you. Instead of the fear of rejection, let me build your trust. It's okay that it's not easy in this season. I know the distance is hard. Your friend is on a journey that's difficult for her, and that has its effects on how she relates to you. But I brought your friendship together and I'll sustain it. The risk to love her again and again, through her change of seasons, is worth taking, just as generously as she has done for you. Be brave and talk to her. Don't hide how you're feeling. Don't let shame lead you. When you share with her, know who you are: a daughter in my family, accepted & embraced. Lean into my arms; I'm staying close. I'll never leave no matter what you do. I love you with all of my heart.

TOOL № 1 : THE HONESTY TOOL

here's my example,

by CHRIS MILLER

It was the day after our annual retreat. Our entire team had just finished hosting more than four dozen men and women. We had loved extravagantly, pouring out from morning to night, leading sessions, making meals from scratch and imparting tools for doing everyday life with the Holy Spirit. I love this retreat. At the end, we gathered as a staff to close the week in prayer and thanksgiving. There we sat, circled up, waiting for the rest of our team to assemble so we could begin our meeting. One of our staff who works alongside me in the media department began to dialogue with me about a work-related matter, needing space to process out loud before moving forward. Tired as I was, I began to verbally process the situation with her, detailing possible options we had in front of us. I noticed my friend Steve listening in, taking in our conversation and responding physically through facial reactions as we outlined possible solutions. Maybe it was because I was tired, and processing some anxiety about the situation, but somehow I knew that Steve wanted to offer his input. I ramped up my internal defense. Just as soon as I had made the choice to close part of myself off, he cut into the conversation and offered his direct opinion and told us what we should do. I put up the wall, rolling my eyes and without a thought or pause, fired a sarcastic shot back at him, "We were having a *conversation* before you sat down." I felt the sting. I pulled up the drawbridge, breaking connection, and began to punish him. I wanted to just walk away, but since I couldn't, I created emotional space. We moved on. We had our staff meeting and I felt sick to my stomach the whole time. I didn't feel justified, I felt guilty. I knew I needed to go process with the Lord.

1 STOP AND ASK

HOLY SPIRIT, WHY WAS MY INTERNAL RESPONSE SO STRONG TOWARD STEVE? WILL YOU COME AND HELP ME UNDERSTAND WHAT'S GOING ON IN MY HEART?

2 GET HONEST

Father, I feel sick to my stomach. I am so frustrated right now. I feel like these moments keep happening between me and Steve and this time I snapped. It wasn't necessary! Why did he force himself into our conversation? I hate being interrupted and I feel like he overpowered me in front of our co-worker. I am not proud of the way I reacted - it just came out of me. Now I feel regret. There is part of me that feels justified - maybe I wanted him to know he was wrong... my pride was hurt. Oh God, would you show me where pride is getting in the way of our relationship? I don't want this moment to become a wedge between us. I care about Steve and value his friendship.

3 REFLECT AND EXCHANGE

I am weak
I am proud
I am interrupted, again
I have to fight to be heard
Conflict is hard

4 LISTEN

Christopher Joel, breathe in deep and receive my peace. Be still... You do not have to rush through this moment. Don't push pain away. True friendship is always worth the fight. Steve is my gift to you - a worthy contender - a brother in arms. You have spent an entire week fighting for others, together. Can you not see? The enemy wants nothing more than to disrupt unity. You both have taken vital ground. It's time to go to a new place of growth in your friendship. I have more for you, and I want to reveal that through this situation. I want to reveal that through others. This is why I have planted you in community. Team is a gift to sharpen and refine you into the man I've called you to be. Don't confuse your pride for justice. I am the only judge of the heart. Have you asked Steve about the moment or have you made an assumption? Humble your heart son. Go to your brother. Open your hands and lower the drawbridge. Your heart longs to be known. Be strong and courageous. My love will lead you back into connection.

LAND IN GRATITUDE

I am a lover of people. I love getting to know their stories. I love sitting with them at the walls they hit and helping them get back up to try again. Being a part of how God changes hearts gives me life, so it is no wonder that I have taken on the role of a pastor. While this work is a joy for me, I confess that knowing how to properly lead people hasn't always come naturally. Finding the balance between loving well while not being overly responsible has been a challenging process. I have learned how to separate others' emotions from my own, trusting the Lord with future outcomes by giving everything back to Him at the end of the day. As I continue to practice, I have discovered how these keys provide a healthy, proactive way for me to have deeper connection with those I am leading and to enjoy the work I am doing each season.

The first key I've learned is to check my emotional temperature. I naturally connect with others through empathy and understanding. This gifting has served me well, but it can also be difficult to navigate. In my early years of leading, when someone would share a story of deep pain with me, I would find myself feeling depressed for days without knowing why. Feeling for people is a beautiful thing until the feelings overshadow the truth. I have struggled for years with letting feelings write the narrative for my thought life, especially in leading others. The Father has taught me the practice of taking my emotional temperature when I start to notice that my normal emotional climate is off. If I am feeling sorrow or irritation after moments of leading, or notice that I am acting rude or withdrawn from those around me, it is a good time to ask the Holy Spirit, "Do I personally need an attitude adjustment or am I still emotionally connected to someone else's process?" This practice helps protect the sacred space of loving others for the gift it is, rather than allowing it to become an overwhelming burden to bear.

The second key is very much connected to the first. The intentional act of giving people back to the Lord is a healthy way of landing the emotions I experienced and submitting them to the Lord. In the "business" of loving and leading, some days can be a lot more challenging than others. Human hearts are messy and sometimes difficult to know how to handle. The Father has taught me how to end a day well by simply slowing down, taking deep breaths and releasing all I was carrying back to Him with gratitude. I pause and recount in simple prayer the moments I had throughout the day, handing the responsibility of those entrusted to me back into His care. A simple prayer like this: "Thank you God for choosing me to be a part of what you are doing in this person's life. I recognize that you are their Father and the Savior of their story. I submit my heart to yours and release this person into your care. Thank you for your perspective of joy and wonder; I receive it now, amen." I not only practice this with those I am leading, but I do it after I lead worship, have a tough day at work or even after a lunch date with a friend. Landing in gratitude puts Jesus on the throne of my life and reminds me that He is God and I am His child. Saving and solving are His responsibilities.

Learning the skill of carrying and loving people well is to learn how to do the Father's work in His way: He gets to be the Savior and I get to partner with Him. While this is never without experiencing the raw messiness of people's process like Jesus did, it should always be full of the fruit of the Spirit and never without hope!

PROMPT: Where might you be trying to carry someone else's story for them? Ask the Father, "Do I personally need an attitude adjustment or am I emotionally connected to their process in an unbalanced way?" Write the Lord's response in your journal. If you find that you have taken responsibility, give that person to the Lord and thank Him for what He is doing in their life.

BY MOLLY SKAGGS

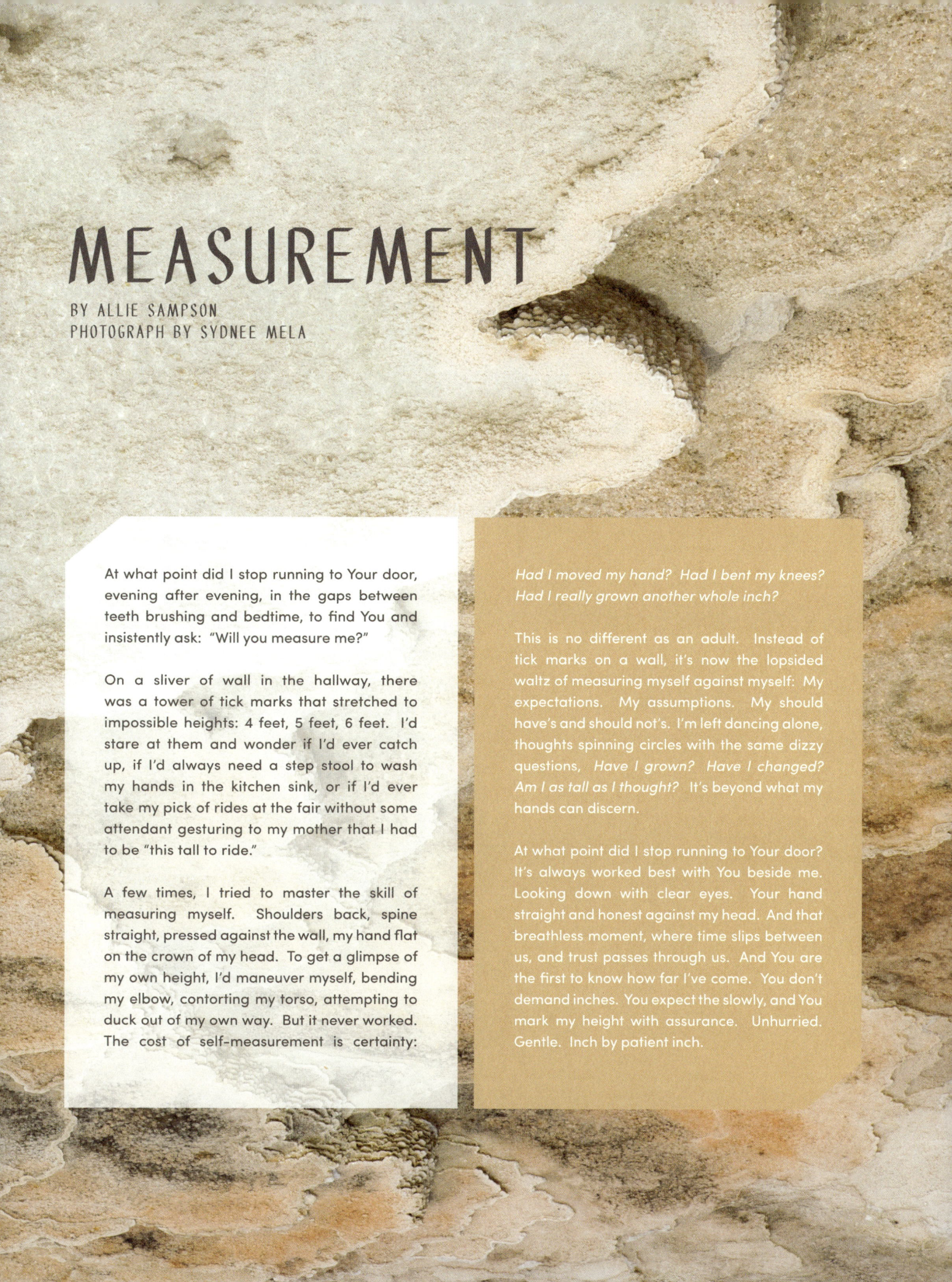

MEASUREMENT

BY ALLIE SAMPSON
PHOTOGRAPH BY SYDNEE MELA

At what point did I stop running to Your door, evening after evening, in the gaps between teeth brushing and bedtime, to find You and insistently ask: "Will you measure me?"

On a sliver of wall in the hallway, there was a tower of tick marks that stretched to impossible heights: 4 feet, 5 feet, 6 feet. I'd stare at them and wonder if I'd ever catch up, if I'd always need a step stool to wash my hands in the kitchen sink, or if I'd ever take my pick of rides at the fair without some attendant gesturing to my mother that I had to be "this tall to ride."

A few times, I tried to master the skill of measuring myself. Shoulders back, spine straight, pressed against the wall, my hand flat on the crown of my head. To get a glimpse of my own height, I'd maneuver myself, bending my elbow, contorting my torso, attempting to duck out of my own way. But it never worked. The cost of self-measurement is certainty:

Had I moved my hand? Had I bent my knees? Had I really grown another whole inch?

This is no different as an adult. Instead of tick marks on a wall, it's now the lopsided waltz of measuring myself against myself: My expectations. My assumptions. My should have's and should not's. I'm left dancing alone, thoughts spinning circles with the same dizzy questions, *Have I grown? Have I changed? Am I as tall as I thought?* It's beyond what my hands can discern.

At what point did I stop running to Your door? It's always worked best with You beside me. Looking down with clear eyes. Your hand straight and honest against my head. And that breathless moment, where time slips between us, and trust passes through us. And You are the first to know how far I've come. You don't demand inches. You expect the slowly, and You mark my height with assurance. Unhurried. Gentle. Inch by patient inch.

Opposites ATTRACT

by JONATHAN HELSER
artwork by MORGAN CAMPBELL

It was in the autumn of 1998 that I looked into Melissa's brown eyes and I was smitten from the first glance.

We fell in love very fast. To be honest, neither of us were supposed fall in love that year. We were first-year ministry school students and we had both made very spiritual plans to take a break from any kind of romantic relationship and spend our time focusing on God. Well, those plans didn't last very long. I had never met anyone like her; she was a whirlwind of passion and beauty, her joy was contagious, her pursuit of God inspiring and did I mention how stunning her brown eyes were? Within a year I placed a ring on her finger and we set a date to be married that spring after we graduated from school. Little did we know how many surprises were waiting to be uncovered in our relationship. One of the most obvious was just how beautifully opposite our personalities actually were. It's incredible how blinded you can be to the truth that "opposites attract" when you are falling in love. One night, on a lovely little date shortly after being engaged, it dawned on us how different we really were. This was such a defining moment for me—I can still vividly remember what everything felt like at this cozy restaurant. We were lost in conversation towards the end of our meal when I slid a question across the table: "What if we inherited a large sum of money in our first year of marriage and we never had to worry about having a job to pay the bills—what would your dream be?"

At this point in our relationship, Melissa had already wisely assessed that I was an internal processor and she had a hunch that I'd been thinking about my response to this question, which she was absolutely correct about. She quickly responded, "You've already been thinking about this. You have to answer first." My eyes got a little dreamy as I looked off into the distance and answered, "My dream would be for us to live in the cliffs of Ireland or Scotland, in a beautiful little cottage surrounded by countryside, overlooking the sea. We would fill our home with musical instruments and spend our days falling in love and making music." Melissa's reaction was not what I was expecting. I had assumed she would love this romantic idea, but she quickly responded with, "Where are the people? I don't want to live alone in some remote countryside." I jokingly answered that we could fulfill God's commission to be fruitful and multiply and we could make some people. She kind of laughed and then honestly said, "I think that dream of yours may be my version of hell!" I nervously laughed off this comment and asked, "Well, what's your dream?" She sat silently for just a moment and then said, "I haven't had as much time to think about it as you, so I'm not sure what my dream destination is, but I do know that I don't want to live alone in the countryside. I want to live in community. We could have a community house…or a school where people could live with us… and our lives would be immersed in community and discipleship." As she finished her response, I replied, "I think your dream may be *my* version of hell." So we did what seemed like the wisest thing possible for two people head-over-heels in love with each other: we decided to get married and figure it out.

Now that we are two decades into this beautiful journey called marriage, we can look back at that night and laugh. We didn't have a clue how different we were from each other. I am more introverted. Melissa is more extroverted. My version of re-energizing is a few hours alone to read or write music. Melissa's way of being refilled is to be with her friends with lots of conversations flowing. I am an internal processor. She is an external processor. I naturally process by being alone in the quiet, where I can think and pray. Melissa's way of processing is to find someone to talk with and work it out in friendship. We are so wonderfully different from one another. I do believe that these differences were the magnetic force that attracted us to each other and that they have also been the cause of a lot of tension in our journey. John Eldredge has an incredible way of describing marriage like a perfect storm. A perfect storm is when two opposite pressure systems meet each other. He illustrates that within this storm, "Our mutual brokenness plays off of each other so perfectly it's frightening. It's like throwing a dog and a cat in a dryer. Why would God do such a thing? Because marriage is a divine conspiracy. God lures us into marriage through many things, then He uses it to transform us."[6]

I have been completely transformed by marriage.

I can clearly see how terrible it would have been for me to live alone in that cottage overlooking the sea, far from community. It could have been easier to just be a musician and never pour myself into community, but I would have missed out on so much. I'm sure that cottage would have been comfortable, but my life would have been boring and my songs would have lacked the depth that can only be found in the process of really loving and being loved by people. There is a leader and pastor inside of me that has emerged over the last twenty years from the beautiful tension of being tethered to my wife's dream. Melissa's passion to love people and invest into their lives has provoked me to love in a way that didn't come intuitively. My natural disposition can be to move away from people, whereas Melissa's instinct is to move towards them. For instance, when Melissa walks into our office she will gravitate towards our staff to offer them her love and her care. My inclination can be the opposite; I can tend to keep to myself and stay focused on my task for the day. While completing tasks is important, if I fail to love and connect with the staff I'm leading, I have missed the most significant thing as a leader. Melissa has taught me to step beyond my natural temperament and move towards the people I am leading. This one adjustment has transformed my leadership, but it has not happened overnight. I still have to practice facing the fears that keep me isolated. One of those fears is that I will not be enough or have enough for everyone in the room. As I've stepped out of what's comfortable and moved towards others in love, I've discovered that the Lord has enough, and this practice has strengthened my trust. It's a common trap to use our personalities as an excuse to avoid engaging what's uncomfortable, but this forfeits growth. I am so grateful for the way I have been challenged by Melissa's differences. I've been inspired to become much more than I could have become by myself.

The same truth applies to Melissa. At the beginning of our relationship, Melissa didn't like being alone. She grew up as the middle of five kids and because being alone was not something she experienced, she was uncomfortable with solitude. My passion for music, creativity and taking time alone for reflection helped to awaken something in Melissa. When we first met, she was not writing or pursuing music. In fact, if you had told us that one day we would record albums together and travel the world playing music, we would've had a hard time believing you. But there was an artist inside of Melissa that could have been buried underneath the busyness of doing good things for others in ministry. She discovered a song inside of her heart through the tension of being tethered to my dream.

For the last twelve years, Melissa and I have pioneered a discipleship school and a full-time community. Last year, we had over ninety staff and students living on our land in North Carolina. Melissa's original dream of discipleship is thriving, but it's not just her dream now—it has become my dream too. The school started very small, with only eight students and just one staff member. Now that our community has grown so much larger, quite a few people ask how we avoid burning out from living in such a full environment. I believe that the key to thriving has been knowing our need for solitude and time alone. We live in a beautiful home that is just a short walk from our school. We don't have students or staff living in our home with us. It's just the two of us, our two children and our two labradoodles. Our community has a tremendous respect for our space and they honor our needs and limits. Although we are not living in a house overlooking the sea, our home is full of instruments and we have had the privilege of making a lot of music in our journey together. Part of my original dream has been fulfilled as well, but it has also become Melissa's dream. She adores the way creativity and solitude restore her soul.

We have both been transformed by each other's differences. I love the way Dietrich Bonhoeffer captures the essence of needing both community *and* solitude to have a full and healthy life:

"Let him who cannot be alone beware of community. Let him who is not in community beware of being alone. Each by itself has profound perils and pitfalls. One who wants fellowship without solitude plunges into the void of words and feelings and the one who seeks solitude without fellowship perishes in the abyss of vanity, self-infatuation and despair."[7]

My hope in sharing some of the tension and beauty of our relationship is to empower you to be challenged and inspired by those who are different than you. I think we all have a natural tendency towards either being introverted or extroverted, just like our right or our left hand is dominant. It would be ridiculous if I decided to stop using my left hand, just because I was more comfortable using my right. I need to use both of my hands to do life to its fullest. I think the same truth applies to our disposition towards solitude and community; we need both to fully enjoy all that God has for us in life. You don't have to be married to experience this gift. All you have to do is choose to move towards people and you will quickly discover how their differences will stretch you and propel you towards growth. In our community, I have seen the introverts inspire the extroverts to enjoy the treasures found in solitude, just as I have seen the extroverts draw out the introverts into experiencing the fullness of friendships.

I love what introverts bring to community when they choose to step beyond what is comfortable. Introverts think brilliant thoughts, but if they never learn to use their voice at the table of community, we miss out on a great treasure. We have challenged our quieter leaders to do the hard work of growing their confidence and this has led them to become some of the most powerful leaders on our team. Introverts have to face their fears when they fully give into community, just as extroverts have to face their fears of being alone when they choose solitude. I love the gifts that extroverts find when they take time away to be still and listen. Some of the greatest artists on our team are extroverts. As our community has practiced rhythms of contemplation and solitude, it has challenged them, but their art would have never been fully unearthed if they hadn't taken the time to find the melodies and words that only the deep parts of their hearts can express. One of the most remarkable truths I have discovered through the perfect storm of marriage and community is: *When I learn to face my fears and step beyond my tendency, I become whole.* My life-long friend Adam Cox says that, "We are found by a Father, but we are formed in a family." May you be inspired to be found by the Father in the moments alone with Him, and may you be provoked to let community transform you into all that God dreamed you to be.

WHEN I LEARN TO FACE MY FEARS AND STEP BEYOND MY TENDENCY,

I BECOME WHOLE.

PROMPT:

Sit down with the Father and ask Him, "Will you speak into my significance? Where have I allowed fear to determine how I relate to community? How can I open up my heart to affect those around me in a powerful way?" Journal His response. Let His truth wash over you and dare to read what He said out loud. Then, reflect on what He said and see what you can begin to practice in your normal life. Perhaps it is speaking up when you have ideas in community moments. Maybe it's risking carving out alone time in your day-to-day life. It could be something that requires you to push past your fears. Whatever it is, choose a friend and share what you found out about yourself and what you're committing to practice.

Apples &

IT'S A MATTER OF APPLES AND ORANGES. You've no doubt heard the saying. When someone uses it we know that what they're getting at is, "I can't answer, there's no comparison. They are fundamentally different." It's kind of the "get out of jail free" card when asked to compare or contrast. In all truth, some things just shouldn't be compared.

Some categories simply cannot be subjected to comparative scrutiny. What is more, we intuitively understand this incomparability with respect to different foods, musical tastes or vacation destinations and really probably most of life's wide array of unique things, experiences and opportunities. But do we ever really extend the logic of "apples and oranges" to ourselves amidst the temptation to compare who we are to others?

Maybe we should.

Comparison isn't innocent like it would like you to think. What starts as a little tempting thought quickly flares up to a face-flushed, pit-in-my-stomach, chest-tight-with-lack, perpetual-monkey-on-my-back type of experience. Comparison gloats that, *I don't have enough, I'm not significant, I'm headed nowhere, I'm too far behind to catch up.* It comes with a firm-fisted grip, telling me to white knuckle the little I have to my name and elbow it away from those who are trying to steal what is mine. Suddenly the success of another only reflects on me, validating the fear that I'm insufficient. Someone else's achievements cannot be celebrated for what they are because they pose a threat to where I am. It tints our vision to a pale, sickly-green envy, seeing others not for who they are but for how they might confirm that our insecurities are true. When comparison applies pressure, the worst of me comes out. Ultimately it fixates my eyes on myself, turns me against others and wants to send me in an isolated, threatened rat race of exhausting measuring up. It's not innocent; comparison wants to take you down.

My mentor, Gabe Valenzuela, once said if you compare yourself to someone else it's always a lose/lose. Either you size yourself up and you "lose"—you come up short, you don't quite measure up and you're left with insecurity, anxiety, a diminished sense of worth. Or worse, you size yourself up against someone and "win"—you are better. You may be better, but the fruit of that thought pattern is pride and arrogance. And that's losing any way you cut it. There's no win in comparison.

Nobody wants to live that way, but how do we get free from it?

First we must understand we are not generating comparison ourselves. We give into it. We can make a practice of listening to and agreeing with it and it will revisit more frequently, beginning to sound like our own thoughts, but it didn't begin with us—no.

The enemy despises the originality of God. Why? Because Satan isn't the maker—"creator" isn't in his capacity or title. He's only a thief; his resumé is ripping things off, making copies and counterfeits. He despises the ability God has to uniquely create, and despises that we stand as a reminder of it. Each uniquely made in His image and one of a kind; mini reminders of His goodness in millions of new expressions.

So what does the enemy do? He tries to convince us that we should be more like someone else, that the gift of our uniqueness is a curse or inconvenience and should be traded for sameness and self-hate. To pit each against the other, neutralizing to a lowest common denominator.

by KALLEY HEILIGENTHAL
photograph by CALEB MARMOLEJO

ORANGES

I'm cliché, I'm not enough, I'm too much, If only I looked, sounded like, acted like, thought more like so and so… The truth is this: comparison isn't firstly an accusation against you. You didn't make you. You're not crafted by your own hand, or dreamt up by your own imagination. No, comparison is an accusation against God as Maker, and the truth is, He's not a maker that makes mistakes. God doesn't make cliché. No one has ever been you before. You were created by an infinite God who only custom-creates and never mass-produces from a factory line. How could you be anything but completely unique and refreshing?

Oftentimes I'll compare myself to someone else and all I ever see is what's on the very surface. I don't know their conversations with God, what their process or journey has been like, the things they've had to fight for and against, and I don't know what God's about to do. I don't even know that about myself.

When we compare, we make ourselves in others' images when we were only made in the image of God. It's been a huge battle for me to learn to appreciate my own singing voice. I had terrible insecurity for years. I negotiated inside that if three people told me my voice was pretty I would believe them and my mind would be changed. Three came and went, and nothing had changed. Like an auctioneer I upped the number over and over but no matter how many people complimented my insecurity, the insecurity wasn't going away. I'd still compare myself to my friends and come up paralyzed.

One day, the Lord quietly interrupted my inner bargaining of self-worth by saying, "You know, you never asked me." "Asked you what?" "Asked me what I think about your voice." All of a sudden I realized my problem wasn't numbers, it was who I was asking. Only the Lord could answer that question in me. So I asked. And He told me, "The Northern Lights dance when you open your mouth, angels spin and nations come together." With tears down my face, I finally felt a deep sense of worth in something I had judged and despised about myself.

So ask Him. And when you ask Him, don't ask like it's a suggestion amidst the other raging voices. Commit to giving Him the loudest spot. Let Him change your mind with whatever He says. Repent for small thinking about yourself and agree with the One whose mouth makes brilliance by simply speaking. He's not lying to you, comparison is. It's not too good to be true. And comparison isn't your friend; it's not keeping you from being rejected or failing. Invite trusted people to speak into who you are, to say what they're seeing, to hold you to it when you stray and to reinforce when you're living in it.

Not only is your personhood and design unique, but your season could be different than those around you, and comparison will only discourage there too. Ask God for a word to live by in your season. Ask how to walk it out well. A friend of mine, Melissa Casey, always encourages people to close their eyes and ask God to show them what their season currently is with a picture of a tree. Is it a winter season? Then maybe your roots are going deep, and the rules to walk your season out will be specific to that process. Maybe the harvest you're planting is for a different kind of fruit, from a different tree, and maybe your tree is in its necessary winter season while your friends seem to be blooming and blossoming. Maybe you're fundamentally different, created masterfully in the heart of a brilliant, endlessly creative Father. Maybe that makes you incomparable, fearfully and wonderfully made. Maybe it really is a matter of apples and oranges.

SPHERES OF INFLUENCE

by LAUREN VALLOTTON / artwork by MORGAN CAMPBELL

THERE'S NO FORMULA FOR RELATIONSHIPS. THEY ARE NOT A ONE-WAY STREET, AND THE MOST INTIMATE PEOPLE IN OUR LIVES ARE LIFE-GIVING AS WELL AS LIFE-TAKING.

Our hearts consistently ask of the people in our lives, *Do you know how to love me well?* When we talk about the intangibles of relationships—things that are so real but hard to pinpoint—it's helpful to have visuals. "Spheres of Influence" is a concept our community has developed and used over the years that has helped us navigate through connecting with people throughout our lives. It refers to a visual diagram of how to think about managing the relationships in your life. It's a picture of a target with a bullseye in the center. Every layer or ring of the target represents a sphere of relationship in your life. In the outermost layer are strangers and acquaintances. As you move from the outer ring into the center, you're increasing in a few different areas: the levels of trust you have with people, commitment levels, intimacy, vulnerability, influence—the influence you have over people and how much they have over you. The center (the bullseye) represents the space in your life you share with the Trinity. You don't share that space with anything or anyone else. This is the "God Spot." It's the epicenter of the whole thing. Our relationship with the Lord is where we find our source for identity. It's the place of ultimate vulnerability, intimacy, healing, provision, protection and trust.

Every person's target is different. For me, my relationship with God is the center. I'm married, so my relationship with my husband is the next ring; he doesn't share a ring with anybody else. Then as I move further out, I have my kids, family and my two best friends. From there I have my friends that I know I can have fun with, then church people that I'm absolutely committed to in community, but I may not have a ton of time and intimacy with them. Then acquaintances and strangers in the outermost ring. Everyone's diagram will look different depending on where you are in life (i.e. married, single, have children, etc.).

Here's the truth: Even if this is a fresh concept to you, you already have this going on. We just need to take inventory. Knowing that all the relationships in our lives have some level of trust, intimacy and vulnerability happening within them, we can take an assessment of who is in our lives and what levels are happening in each relationship. That's where we begin. Simultaneously, as we learn our healthy boundaries, expectations and the needs in our lives and relationships, those considerations help us see if we place people appropriately.

Now, I don't have a poster on my bedroom wall with stickers and magnets of each person in my life; I don't move people around consciously and assign them to rings. Spheres of Influence is a sort of internal compass. I've never had conversations with people saying, "Hey, just wanted to let you know that you are in my Level 2 Ring." The reality is we do need to take a self-assessment, because we'll be much more effective in our relationships if we intentionally take time to assess and ask, *What levels of trust, intimacy, vulnerability, connection, commitment and influence do I have with the people in my life? Is he or she in my God Spot?* Thinking through those questions might reveal that you've put someone in the God Spot, relying on him or her for your source of identity.

This concept is not about exclusivity or inclusivity; it's really about protecting love. We're all wired differently by God, with different capacities. It's not true to say, "Oh, twenty people is way too many relationships to have in that ring." No, you have a capacity that maybe others don't have. The whole point is to protect the core—nothing should damage our ability to protect our relationship with the Trinity. We have to gain a lot of grace and understanding with people who are different than us. It's important to consider the boundaries you have. Boundaries exist to protect our capacity to love people. Sometimes people abuse boundaries. They feel like, *Are you trying to keep me away with your boundary?!* It's up to me—based on how I'm wired, my own capacities, my priorities, the season of life I'm in, etc.—to figure out how I love the people in my world. How do I love my husband? The church person? The friend I'm in Small Group with? Some boundaries are set up by default. For example, there are things I share with my husband only that wouldn't be appropriate to share with anybody else. On the other hand, there are other boundaries that we must set up with more intentionality.

An example of moving people toward the center of my target: I have some girl friends from home who had grown up with me. We were deeply committed to one another in friendship and had beautifully grown in intimacy over the years. They were in my "Ring 2"—the friends who shared hearts with me. But when I flew across the country to be a student at Bethel, then married Jason, moved officially to Redding to work at Bethel Church and put down roots in this city, the more I realized that those long-distance friendships weren't enough. For a little while we were able to sustain each other's needs for close friendship, but the more that I put down roots in the city, the harder it got to stay connected. God designed the body to function together, and I needed friends that I could touch, see, work with, rub shoulders with. As deep as my friendships were with my friends from home, I started to recognize a deep void in my life. I needed friendships that reached deeper than just having fun together. In that season I was learning to be a wife and a parent for the first time. My heart was longing for relationships with women I could touch and see in my daily life who could share this season with me. So, I started drawing closer to a couple of women in my city who I knew I could trust with my heart. We had the same core values and were in a similar season of life. We intentionally started meeting together and formed a Small Group, and for the past five years they've been my closest friends in Redding. I can't imagine doing life without them. They came into my life because I recognized a deep need, *Oh, I'm lacking an entire Third Ring of friendships!*—and I figured out how to meet that need.

On the opposite end of the spectrum, around the same time, I had a friend from back home who I felt like I was failing. I was disappointing her all the time. I hate disappointing people! I thought, *Oh, man. I have to deal with this in a healthy way. I don't want to push my friend out and build a wall between us.* A boundary is not the same thing as a wall. I wanted to love my friend well, but I knew that communicating my honest feelings would hurt. I realized I didn't have the capacity or even the desire to continue in our level of friendship. With learning how to be a wife and mom in my new season, I was totally maxed out! I couldn't even be a good friend to the person down the road, let alone my friend two-thousand miles away. I wasn't doing a good job of keeping connected. I had to figure out, *What are my needs? Why do I feel like I'm failing?* Honestly, what it came down to was she had expectations of me in our friendship that I was continually not meeting. Expectations that go unmet lead to pain. I ended up calling her and saying, "Hey, I love you and respect you a lot, so I need to have this conversation with you. I want to do a great job loving you, but you have expectations of me that I can't meet, so you're in pain about it. And that's causing me pain. I'm going to do a much better job of loving you if we change the expectations a bit. Could we…?" Essentially, I had to communicate what I could and couldn't do. We are still friends to this day, and I love her dearly, but our friendship has changed since we moved each other to an outer ring.

There's no cookie cutter way around this concept. We're talking about people's hearts! And while the diagram language is helpful, this isn't as simple as a poster on a wall. The lines are a lot harder to draw than we make them sound sometimes. At the end of the day, navigating through this diagram is about self-awareness. You must know yourself first. You can't receive love if you don't have any needs and if you can't express them. It won't matter how hard other people try, you won't feel loved. Start by developing the ability to communicate your needs. May we all grow in learning ourselves, and find peace in discovering God in our "God Spot."

PROMPT: Take a moment with the Lord to consider your Spheres of Influence. Ask and pray, "Lord, I want you to be in my God Spot. Help me to turn to you solely as my source for ultimate intimacy, protection, provision and trust. Show me the relationships that are the most influential in my life right now and how I can steward them with love and boundaries." Journal His voice.

PRACTICE: Make a list of your closest friends. Are there ten, three, none? As you look at the list, assess with the Holy Spirit and ask, "Am I stewarding this relationship with love and boundaries?" Allow yourself time to hear His response. It may be time to move a person closer or outside of the ring they are in. Ask yourself, *Is this person trustworthy? Do they belong in this ring?* Let this new understanding inspire you to make powerful choices for you and your friendships.

DIGGING A LITTLE DEEPER

Helpful questions to steward your relationships.

Is God in my God Spot or is someone else there? What new boundaries do I need to put in place to protect my connection with God?

Are there people in my life that know the deepest parts of me? Have I taught these people how to love me well?

Is there someone in my outer ring that I've built trust with that I'd like to move closer? Is there someone in an inner ring that I need to move into an outer ring?

PEACE MAKING

by TERESA ARCHER — artwork by JUSTINA STEVENS

"In but not of, in but not of, in but not of…" It feels like decades that I have whispered this under my breath, full of concern, wonder, resilience, hope, in different locations as I have questioned what Jesus meant when He prayed for me before entering Gethsemene.

What were the specifics in His heart that He hoped we would live with, full of communion with Holy Spirit as we walked not away, but into, the world around us? As He asked for us to remain, and engage—"Don't hide, don't separate, don't undercut, don't decimate, but rather go in and bring me with you."

What does it mean to be a child of the Father as you walk through the doors of industry, unhelpfully termed "the system" by those of us who take jobs and employment in arenas we are less than inclined to pursue were it not for the need to provide for ourselves and our family? There are so many principles of partnership, and culture, that the Kingdom of Heaven operates in, but I have moved from world to world and found one guiding role that has challenged me the most. As I transitioned from a Christian high school to a liberal arts college, from The Cheesecake Factory to the world of art auctioneering, from a personal assistant to a recording artist and songwriter, to my role as head editor of a media company, it has always been a fight to lay down my own desire to succeed and embrace the line, "Blessed are the peacemakers, for they shall be called sons of God" (Matthew 5:9, ESV).

Peacemaking is strident. It takes more energy and utilizes more stamina than living in a state of war. Even the language—to make peace—is active. It implies that we must employ our creativity, that we must bring something in that otherwise wouldn't exist, and the history of humanity itself attests to this fact. Jesus called us to make, form and produce peace in the world. We are to bring the King's gift out of the invisible and into the natural space. Yet often what we settle for as peace can be false, mistaking a lack of external conflict or a simmering quiet around us for peace.

In my last workplace, there was a moment where nearly everyone working as department heads had known one another for a long time. There was a running harmony, like a playful tune, constantly bubbling around the office, and my role was—for the most part—easy to execute, as I ran creatively. Then one day, a new hire walked into the office and it was as though someone had introduced a tuba player to a string quartet. This woman was holding an entry-level position in our company, but because we were small, both her attitude and her presence were hard to ignore. She boldly declared her hatred (and that was the word) for spirituality, mocked women who embraced conservative values and carried a chip a mile high on her shoulder. I was shocked that she was chosen to enter our sanctuary—the office space that was, in my mind, a bastion of encouragement. I bristled. Externally, I looked like a casual observer, neither interested nor disgusted by what she was saying. Internally, I reacted. I was in disagreement with every word she was saying. When she wrote her first article proposal weeks later, I communicated back to her in as brusque a style as she spoke, which was not really my normal when I responded to writers. I decided to do my job in as "professional," almost robotic, way as possible. I basically threw my critiques in her face, treating her as unkindly as she was treating others.

The day after I did so, I saw her meeting with our office manager, in tears. My heart hit my shoes as that horrible taste shot up into my mouth. It was all a grand facade. Bluster. She had been posturing, showing a brave face and I had missed it in my high-handed desire for office ease. I was ignoring the clear signs of a woman in pain and acting instead as a victim, when I was one of the only people enabled by my relationship with Holy Spirit to actually bring a salve to her wounds. I had "kept my peace," but I had not made peace. The Father began to speak to me about her, and as she ranted about politics or spit obscenities about certain belief systems, tiny pieces of who she really was and how she had experienced life began to fall out of her. She had been horribly abused. She was drinking heavily to anesthetize. Her relationship with her mum was strained. Her parents never gave her Christmas presents. Instead of hearing what she was saying, I began to listen to the heart of God as He poured out His compassion for her. You see, I discovered that I had been paying attention to the wrong thing—her behavior. I had gotten side-tracked from my role as a child of the Father by the fact that she had disturbed what was a humming, fairly quiet office environment.

Deep peace can't be removed by the presence of someone bringing the world in with them. Deep peace resides within us—the gift of Holy Spirit, who Jesus promised us would override "the troubles of this world." I befriended this sweet woman and began to reach out with small responses of compassion and actually listen for the moments that were an entryway to real connection. She changed a lot, and so did I. I was leading her to where real peace resides, without hiding myself or my convictions, even sharing sometimes how my family relates together, where we fail and how those hurts really aren't reflecting God's desires for us. She gave up drinking one month before her birthday, and I sent her a bottle of non-alcoholic spirits to keep in her home for special occasions. She told me the next day she cried with the thoughtfulness of it. I was finally making peace with her, and it looked like intimacy.

Fighting for peace in the atmospheres around us requires so much. Just as in every area of our lives, we must remain awake and alert, watchful and ponderous as we relate to others. One of the deepest secrets to unlocking carrying true peace must be to walk in integrity of heart, mind and mouth. I watch for moments when, in discussing something from my day, I say to my husband, "I don't even care." That phrase is like a flashing red light yelling "*STOP* and go no further!" It's a signal flare that I've given up on a fight inside of myself. I am like my Father, and my Father is all caring and passion. The first step to checking in on if I have abdicated my role as a creator of peace, is to ask the Holy Spirit as I am interacting with others, "Holy Spirit, why am I so unsettled or so apathetic?" The second step is to ask myself, *What do I really believe about this situation?* As soon as I hear the words "hopeless," "ruined," "impossible," or anything like these, I know that I have forgotten the power and gift that the Father has given me to walk in His authority. I don't mean the kind of authority that steps in and takes over with forceful words or arguments, but rather the kind that sacrifices self for love and honor.

When I bring my frustrations and my worries concerning the everyday life of working with others to my time with the Father, He speaks to me of those individuals in such a way that I and my mindset are transformed. I'm no longer afraid to tell the truth about how I feel, or my feelings themselves change. I don't stand up for truth "because it's the right thing" when a conflict arises, but rather Truth is a person and a way that I live inside of. It's so a part of me because it's my bloodline, my right of inheritance. I am a child of God—I am co-creating peace with Him.

> Peacemakers never give up, never believe it's too late, always bear all things, believe all things, endure all things and hope all things. Peacemakers are lovers of God.

Every day, we have the opportunity to either coast through our lives or to look at the war of the worlds inside of us and outside and decide with joyful determination, "I'm in this." We show up, not worried about how we might be hurt, but ready to go to the mat for love and for honesty, no matter the cost, in any conversation we have, small or large. It's exhilarating and hard work, bringing the fullness of what we are learning about redemption to every area of our lives, but well worth it. Peacemakers never give up, never believe it's too late, always bear all things, believe all things, endure all things and hope all things. Peacemakers are lovers of God.

PRAYER: Father, help me to see where my everyday has become so routine that I have forgotten to invite you into it. Help me to show up fully, to care with your heart for those around me and to believe for radical change. Right now, I ask that you show me an area that I have lost tenderness in—and restore in me a soft heart. Take me on a journey to learn what it means to be a peacemaker like you.

Rejecting Comparison

by LINDSAY VANCE

FRIENDSHIP IS THE MEETING OF TWO UNIQUE EXPRESSIONS OF GOD; GOD LIVING INSIDE OF YOU MATCHED WITH GOD LIVING INSIDE OF ME.

It is a canvas for unparalleled originality. One friendship was never meant to mirror another. This is a truth that has taken me the last decade to wrestle through. I've had a habit of holding my own friendships up to the light of other friendships—our honesty to their honesty, our silliness to their silliness, our vulnerability and beauty to theirs. I've experienced disappointment and loneliness because I put demands on my friends and I put demands on myself: *be like someone else*.

There is a pair of close friends that I admire greatly. I sense the deep affection they share simply in the way they say "hi" to one another. At the same time, they have this ability to erupt into sheer silliness; laughing uncontrollably and making everyone around them want to join in the fun. Their friendship is magnetic. I've oftentimes found myself desiring a closeness in friendship like theirs. Can you relate to that desire? Here's where it became painful: I let my desire for a close friend turn into comparing all of my friendships to that one ideal. I struggled with diminishing all of the qualities that set my friends and I apart. Instead of letting thanksgiving lead me in a celebration of our own closeness, my judgment clouded my ability to openly give and receive the beauty that was uniquely ours.

"Compare" can be defined as "to be of an equal or similar nature or quality."[8] Within friendship, comparison is a thief. It robs our ability to enjoy people for who they truly are. It limits our ability to enjoy ourselves, and ultimately, our connection with the Father. God has hidden His likeness inside every human heart, yet not one of us is the same. When we try to make two people alike, it strips away God's vision for a person's life, their God-given identity, causing us to elevate our own vision for their life above the Lord's. It steals God's abundance, creativity and potential for connection between two people, demanding that another person be equal to or of a similar nature to someone else. Not only is that unattainable, it's a total affront to the Kingdom. Paul warns us against comparison when he writes to the Galatians: "That means we will not compare ourselves with each other as if one of us were better and another worse. We have far more interesting things to do with our lives. Each of us is an original" (Galatians 5:26, MSG).

So how do we live within the reality where "each of us is an original"? Instead of following the voice of comparison, we have to listen for the voice of God. He knows us and our friends better than we do. Through His gateways of compassion and affection, He confidently leads us into friendships that nourish us, challenge us and make us more like Him.

There are still days when comparison seeks to direct my thoughts, and I get lost in the refrain of "not enough" and "too much." Rejecting comparison has required that I get honest with what I really believe about myself so that God can exchange my thoughts for His own. I have been met over and over by a God who enjoys me. When I let His affection wrap around my worthiness, I am much more likely to extend love, compassion and understanding to my friends. I can receive them for who they truly are and not what I want them to be for me.

Rejecting comparison has also required that I pay attention to my feelings and practice new thought patterns. I've recognized that when I start to feel sorry for myself or become judgmental towards others, comparison is often dictating my thoughts. Instead of obsessing over what I wish I had, I've learned to catch the cycling thoughts and reflect on the gift of my friendships. This often looks like me taking a deep breath, finding my friends in the room and remembering how I've experienced genuine connection with them. My self-talk sounds something like this: *Hannah loves when I come close to her. I know I have a seat beside her. Allie responds wholeheartedly to my greeting every morning. She welcomes me. Morgan gets my jokes. I want to make her laugh today. Emily goes out of her way to connect with me, even when I'm busy. I want to initiate a special time with her this week.* This simple practice has generated peace and gratitude in my everyday relationships.

God is showing me that I will never come to the end of Him inside my friends. He's revealing that an ideal friendship could never be as good as the real thing, one that's overflowing with permission, caught up in the ebb and flow of the Holy Spirit's leading. The result is a deep satisfaction of feeling known and delighted in.

PROMPT: Ask the Holy Spirit to highlight a friendship that has been affected by your own comparisons. In what ways is He asking you to trade in your perception of "not enough" or "too much" for His perspective? Journal His voice. Then, with this new perspective, write a prayer of thanksgiving for both the powerful and subtle ways this friend has affected your life. Practice this reality when you next spend time with your friend.

SECTION 02

COMMUNICATION

"...BUT INSTEAD LET YOUR WORDS BECOME BEAUTIFUL GIFTS THAT ENCOURAGE OTHERS, DO THIS BY SPEAKING WORDS OF GRACE TO HELP THEM."
EPHESIANS 4:29

by MELISSA HELSER | photograph by SYDNEE MELA

I LOVE LEADING WORSHIP. IT HAS BROUGHT ME IMMENSE JOY. BUT I BURN FOR PASTORING AND BUILDING TEAM.

Jonathan and I have different loves and have both given into the dream of learning to support each other. We've given into growing in the areas that we were weak in. I started writing songs because my husband loved writing songs and Jonathan started leading a team because I loved leading a team. We have learned to lead together and, in that beautiful quest, have fallen in love with leading in all aspects. We are twenty years into marriage, leading schools, camps, worship, team, parenting and community, all at the same time. From the beginning, we felt really aware that this was the Lord's dream. We never wanted it to become the Jonathan and Melissa show. We knew that if we tried to carry this dream on our own, we would absolutely be on a fast track to burn out. We wanted to be in it for the long haul. We craved team—people we didn't just lead, but people who could run with us; alongside us. We didn't just want to build a community, we wanted to carry a dream *with* community and *in* community. Unified in a mission together.

In my opening to this book, I talked about values. Here, I'm going to unpack them deeper. What does it mean to lead people beyond rules into a healthy Kingdom culture, one where you work hard and dream hard? Where the words of Jesus are your guiding compass for how to lead people and you experience seasons of growth and seasons of hardship knowing that every season makes you stronger. My desire is to unpack the power of team and to give you keys on how to create a healthy team or refine the one you have. This isn't just about leading team in ministry, it's about leading any team. We have had the unique privilege of weaving in and out of ministry and business. This tension has been a huge blessing for us. It has forced us to ask good questions and practice refining as a cultural norm.

When I read the Sermon on the Mount, I see Jesus flipping a rule-based culture on its head and implementing a completely different perspective, one that is driven by a deeper value system. One that focuses on the transformation of the inner man. One that asks better questions about motives and belief systems. A perspective that takes us beyond a performance and striving culture into a deeper maturity and accountability before the Lord. It wasn't that what He was teaching was easier. It actually felt impossible. Instead, He was introducing a new way of thinking that takes us beyond behavioral management to real maturity. He knew we would never be able to accomplish any of it without the Cross and Resurrection and Infilling of the Holy Spirit. He gave us access to Himself and that makes all the difference. He introduced a newness and then walked it out with His disciples every day. It wasn't perfect. It was real life, and He loved it.

We get asked all the time how we built a thriving community, and I consistently say: "Very slowly. One person at a time." It started with one intern. Then three. Then a few more each year, who eventually became our staff. I know now that those first few years were a really value-driven time; it was about forming a culture. We wanted to create a Kingdom culture, which can't be done through rules and guidelines but through planting values inside of people's hearts. Our first five years were constant value-centering. Jonathan and I were in a process of discovering our values. We had to constantly evaluate and decide, "This is what we want, this is what we don't want. This is what works, this is what doesn't." We sat with our small staff and chose to be intentional with them. Some values, we imparted. Others, we had to wrestle out. This process is how we have built everything, staying centered in grace and mercy and requiring a commitment to maturity. I am going to unpack a few of our core values. The most important thing is not that you implement *our* values, but that you ask the Lord, "What are *my* values?" Asking questions should be normal for any environment. It is vital that you and your team, whether that be your family, co-workers, staff, etc., learn to ask good questions with no shame. An environment of good questions is an environment that is constantly growing.

COMMITMENT TO PERSONAL GROWTH

In Matthew 22:37 (NIV), Jesus responds to the question, "What is the most important commandment?" He states, "'Love the Lord your God with all your heart and with all your soul and with all your mind.' This is the first and greatest commandment. And the second is like it: 'Love your neighbor as yourself.'" I would consider this the most important core value we have—the belief that, "I'm going to love you to the degree that I love myself." Our staff is committed first to the transforming work of becoming like Jesus; not a lofty religious idea of wholeness, but a healthy commitment to the ongoing work of personal transformation. Over the last ten years, this has worked itself out through implementing emotional health into our culture. "Emotional health" is a hot word right now, but it was absolutely a saving grace for us. We taught self-awareness without self-obsession. How can we love our neighbor if our rhythms of loving self are neglect, coping, diminishment, self-preservation, pride and so on? We started to put in place self-reflecting tools that appropriately required our staff to show up for themselves. They had to learn how to tend to their own hearts with Jesus and not just lean on their leaders to figure it out for them. The Honesty Tool was one of the main game-changing tools (see pg. 42).

We started seeing a dramatic shift in our staff after seasons of practicing honesty and vulnerability before the Lord. The addition of a simple tool where they could get alone with the Father, Son and Holy Spirit and sift through their emotions, behaviors and thoughts, and then write an honest prayer was life changing. They were able to get a handle on the lies they were believing, make a trade and journal His voice. It formed, and is still forming within them, a commitment to the work of Salvation, and they are experiencing the reward of submission to Jesus. For me, it's way more valuable to know that my team is submitted to the Lord and His love and correction, than to know that they're submitted to me. I do not want an environment where I am in control of my staff. I want an environment where Jesus is King. I learned early on that we have to be taught how to cultivate our inner world. Jonathan and I began to love sitting with our staff after they had done the work. We started feeling the reward of intentionality. They knew we weren't going to work harder than them, but we also weren't going to leave them alone to do the work of maturing. Every aspect of loving the Lord, loving yourself and loving your neighbor is dovetailed together. I know that my staff are always growing and learning. We don't arrive, we just keep going. It's unrealistic for me to expect my staff to arrive and never need help again. Every season requires a newness of surrender to the Lord and to the process.

COMMITMENT TO GROWTH IN RELATIONSHIP

Along with the addition of self care, we asked a lot of questions about how to love one another well. I would definitely say that our old belief system was that any kind of tension was bad, and we were doing really well if there were no fights and everyone just got along. We couldn't have been further from the truth. Without tension you cannot play music; too much tension and the strings break, but not enough tension and no sound will come out. I love how many times we see glorious tension in the process of Jesus walking with His boys. He was never put off by their humanity. He constantly taught them, corrected them, asked them questions and challenged their thinking. The key is that He did all of it rooted and grounded in love. There is a responsibility for my staff to learn to listen to and love feedback from leadership and there is an even greater responsibility for leadership to be submitted to the Love of Christ. It isn't one or the other; it's both. My staff has grown to love and crave feedback because they know I love them and will lay down my life for them. When I bring correction, I also remind them, "This is a 5% moment. The 95% of your life is incredible, but this 5%, if unchecked and not addressed, will grow."

This has gone beyond just leadership. They have learned to walk this out with each other. We value tension, conflict and honesty. We believe that there is a reward on the other side of healthy conflict and that reward is connection. We want real relationships that are full of grace and compassion. To have a healthy, thriving work environment as well as a healthy community environment, we have had to go beyond a "forgive and forget" mentality. We have had to teach our staff how to work out their differences, own their mistakes and ask for forgiveness. We have all learned how to listen to each other with open hands and do the work to receive the reward of unity. We actually disagree a lot as a team and I am thankful that it doesn't derail us. The communication tool that we put in this book is part of our community's actual daily practicing tools. We use them, we refine them and we practice them with each other. We have rhythms of clean fighting, listening well, checking our tone and body language, saying sorry and not expecting perfection. All of these practices have made our team and environment a safer place to work and thrive.

GRATITUDE

When my kids were little and they would completely meltdown over something silly, like not getting a piece of candy or not getting to do something they really wanted to do, I would ask them to say five things they were thankful for. It would always pull them out of their overly self-focused swirl and perspective would return. It's funny how it also works with adults. We get tired and selfish and overwhelmed. We convince ourselves that we are all alone and no one wants to help, that everything Jesus has asked us to do is too hard and we are incapable of doing it. The dark clouds arrive and in a hot second, my staff are spinning out of control. Here enters the scene of a Gratitude Break. We just start thanking the Lord out loud, which usually turns into singing, and in a few minutes, we have perspective back. Psalm 100:4 (MSG): "Enter with the password: 'Thank you!' Make yourselves at home, talking praise. Thank him. Worship him." I love that Jesus thanked His Father before every miracle. Create an atmosphere of gratitude and you will have an atmosphere of Heaven.

LAYING DOWN OUR LIVES FOR THE GOSPEL

Having a mission, in my opinion, was such a fast track of maturing for the disciples. They had a consistent outreach, a consistent pouring out. And then they would pull away together. I love the moments when Jesus was with the thousands and then He pulled back into being with the twelve, spending time with them, explaining parables, cooking meals on a beach and answering silly questions like, "How many times am I going to have to forgive?" His love was resilient and it was also patient. Over and over He taught them how to see the world, see people, see the Kingdom. My team's growth is so important. Growth takes time. It takes commitment. It takes a willingness to communicate, often more than once. And it happens most powerfully when it's hand-in-hand with a mission that's greater than themselves. It is so important that your team feels the deep value of mission. No matter what kind of team you lead. This is the thing that we are all committed to, that is bigger than ourselves. It's about teaching our team to not get overly self-focused and to look outward. We want to be driven by the way Jesus washed His disciples' feet and invited us into the same posture of becoming great by bowing low and serving. Having a mission-driven culture has kept us focused on the greater vision, which is laying down our lives for the world.

DREAMING AND DOING

We sat at dinner with a friend who's also a leader. I remember the beauty of discussing and trading keys, sharing all that we'd collectively learned over the years. What I remember most is when we asked him how he creates an environment of getting things done without anxiety. He answered, "My team knows they don't have to perform, but they do have to produce." We loved it and pocketed it for our own growing culture. It's not enough to just dream big dreams if they don't actually materialize. Just like it's not enough to have an apple tree if it doesn't produce apples. We are a culture of dreaming really big and then working really hard. We affectionately call it "Joyful Go Mode." This is the mode we all shift into to get things done, but with joy and honor for each other. We practice never sacrificing our relationships on the altar of accomplishments, while we also practice extreme focus and working hard to hit deadlines. Again, it's not one or the other; it's both.

PEOPLE OVER FUNCTION

This is the value where we let go of the lust for a perfect team that doesn't require ongoing work. As leaders, we must accept the journey of loving people and understand that there is no perfect team. People will continue to make mistakes and continue to need care. I love that at the end of the three years Jesus walked intimately with Peter, Peter completely stalled out and betrayed Him. It broke Jesus' heart, but He was committed to the person. He called him to the shore, restored his heart first and then restored his function. Jesus is a brilliant leader.

We know we are first committed to people and human hearts over anything. In our team, we are all committed to each of us becoming whole. We are all in it for the long haul. I have learned that when I commit to a person, give them tools and teach them how to use those tools appropriately, their function oftentimes locks into place. I don't have to rail them on being better; they want to become better because they feel believed in.

I have also learned that giving authority away too soon because someone is highly gifted can be really dangerous. Maybe they are ready in their gifting, but they aren't ready emotionally or spiritually to do what we are asking them to do. It's easy to invest into people's function and not really commit to their inner world, the character and beauty of who they are without their gifting. At the end of the day, people are the reward. Function and gifting will always come second.

The greatest privilege is loving human hearts. This is what Jesus modeled for us, choosing twelve and loving them with everything He had, with no reservations. He picked the ones that He knew came with mess. They all had different stories, propensities, opinions and outlooks on life and still, He chose them and committed Himself fully to loving them. Remember, leadership is not just about assembling a team that you don't have to do any work with. That's not what Jesus modeled for us. It's about getting values in place that people can grow into. Everyone wants to grow. As leaders, it's our job to keep reminding them that they have what it takes to be amazing and they have what it takes to commit to the process of growth. It's our job to carry the same love in our eyes that the disciples saw when they looked at Jesus.

PROMPT: I encourage you to not overthink this but go into it with an open heart and open mind. The Holy Spirit wants to help you become an amazing leader. Values are essential in every environment whether that be home, work or ministry. Take time to ask yourself these questions—What are the values of our team? Does everyone clearly know what those values are? Do they feel the weight of commitment to growth? Do they know we are committed to their whole person and not just to their function? Are they confident that we will speak truth to their face, assertively and in love? Do they get excited about feedback and refining? Is everyone committed to growth, each person knowing that they have a responsibility to continue maturing with God?

styles
of communication

by CHRIS AND JESSIE MILLER
artwork by JUSTINA STEVENS

PASSIVE   ASSERTIVE
AGGRESSIVE   PASSIVE-AGGRESSIVE

Have you ever had a moment with a friend, a spouse or a co-worker that ended with you saying or thinking, "That is not what I meant," or, "I can't believe they thought that about me!" Where do these misunderstandings come from? What's happening in those moments? It's easy to blame other people when oftentimes, the true source of frustration is rooted in our own communication style—the way we say things.

As a community, we believe that healthy communication is worth fighting for and are very aware of the time and intentionality it takes to cultivate. Language is a gift from God and He longs to see us using it in ways that produce thriving relationships. We honor Him when we use our words to cultivate connection with each other. But, we know what it's like to mean well—to want to love like Jesus and find yourself really struggling—wondering, *Is it supposed to be this hard?* Learning to be vulnerable—to be brave and risk opening up to another person—is essential for maintaining connection in your relationships. But most of us were never taught how to do it well. We want to empower you with tools designed to help find out *what* you need to share to keep your connections strong. But first, we want to illuminate *how* you are prone to say these things. If you rush into vulnerability, unaware of what your communication style is projecting, you can cause a lot of damage. We want to offer you help on how to engage people in a healthy, powerful way.

Your tone, posture and mode of speaking all work together to form your communication style. Every one of us has inherited tendencies that have been heavily influenced by the environments we grew up in. Most of us are unaware of how deeply we have been affected and why we feel reactive in our relationships. Did you grow up in a family that employed shouting to make a point or win an argument? Were you raised in an environment that avoided confrontation at all costs? Did confrontation look like subtle comments and snide remarks? Chances are, by this point in your life, you've experienced and employed some form of every unhealthy communication style: aggressive, passive and passive-aggressive.

We want to bring awareness and understanding to how these three styles damage connection and invite you into pursuing the only effective style: assertive communication. Assertive communication seeks to understand and is rooted in value, for yourself and others. The phrase "I matter, you matter" has become a standard for how our community approaches one another. Learning how to communicate your needs and desires in life without sabotaging your relationships is a part of working out your salvation.

As you read through each of these sections, consider how your use of the negative styles affects your ability to connect with others. More than likely you have used a combination of all three. Maybe you get really aggressive around your family, but feel so passive at work. Perhaps you jab your husband passive-aggressively while passively hiding your feelings with your friends. Ask the Holy Spirit to reveal yourself to *you*. He wants to bring awareness to how unhealthy patterns of communication have kept you stuck in unfruitful or toxic cycles of conversation for years. He is with you, ready to inspire you with a new way to approach connection.

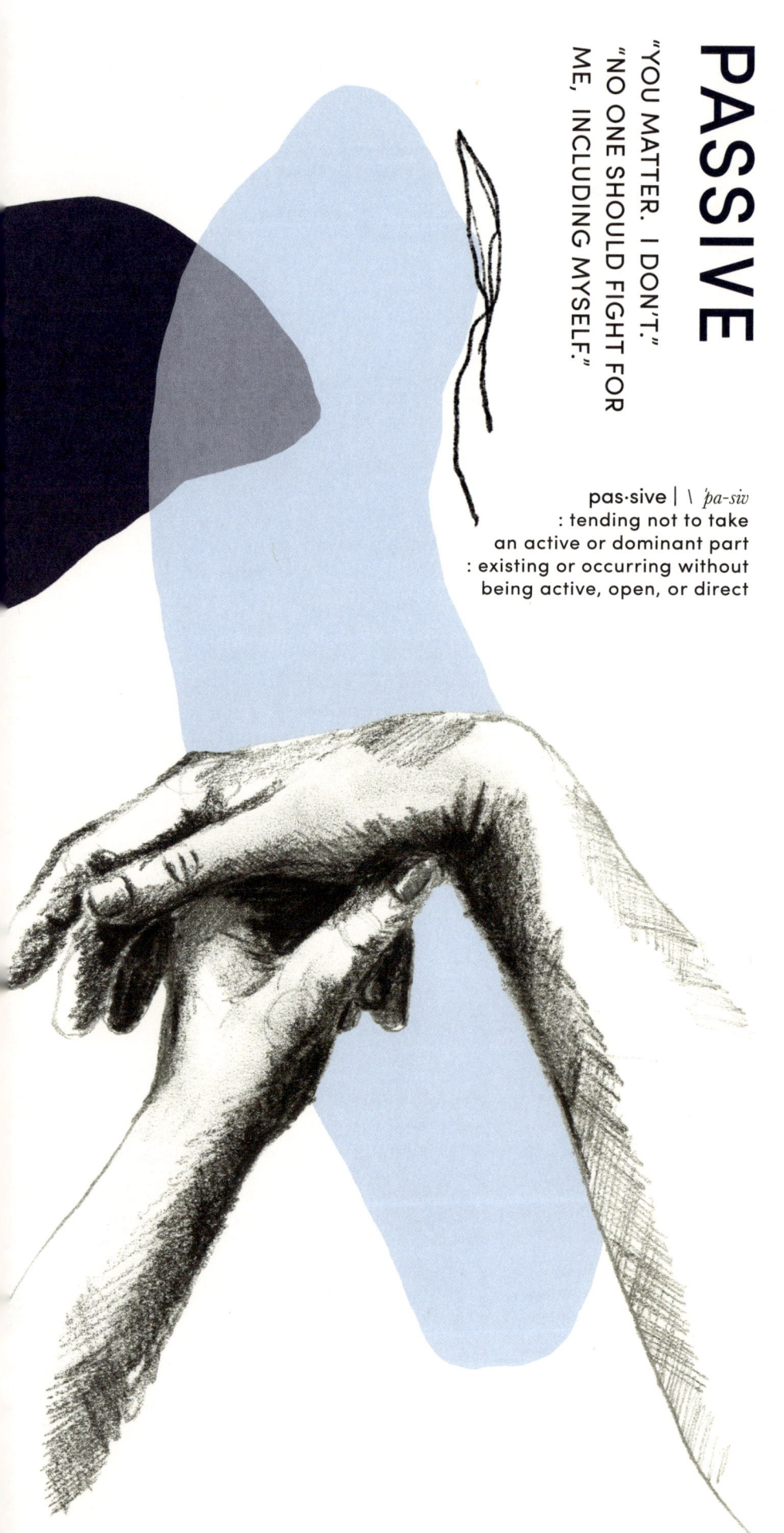

PASSIVE

"YOU MATTER. I DON'T."
"NO ONE SHOULD FIGHT FOR ME, INCLUDING MYSELF."

pas·sive | \ *'pa-siv*
: tending not to take an active or dominant part
: existing or occurring without being active, open, or direct

Has anyone ever said to you, "You're so quiet," or, "Wow, you're so nice, nothing bothers you!" Have you found yourself anxious at the thought of expressing something personal—or anything at all? While listening to others, do you find yourself afraid you won't know what to say, certain no one will ever understand you?

People communicating in this style perceive a fear of not being valuable or heard as an excuse to not try—starting sentences they don't finish, not telling anyone their needs or how things affect them, and gravitating towards a lack of eye contact, the shuffling of feet or even insincere smiles. Passive communicators tend to internalize everything—struggling to vocalize what they are feeling—and then default to, "I'm wrong, you're right," or, "I'll give in…" when working through tension with another person. This style is quick to take blame in the moment by either shutting down, saying nothing or quickly apologizing—anything to get them out of the tension. It is a false attempt to make others feel valuable by devaluing themselves.

Passive communication is painful because it almost always leads to resentment and entitlement in relationships. It puts extreme amounts of pressure on others to "figure you out." Resentment builds as you lean into the assumption that, *Surely they know how this is affecting me.* Entitlement feels reasonable—*I know what they want; they should figure out what I want!* Passive communicators typically reach a point where their feelings and needs finally overtake their desire to hide them and they snap—often in a very painful or confusing blow up. They hear things like, "Well gosh, I never knew you felt that way!" or, "But that happened so long ago, what does that have to do with this?" Hiding your feelings can really damage trust in a relationship, sending the message that the other person doesn't care about you and will always fail you.

Not all passive communicators are quiet or reserved. The use of smiles, jokes and happy language can be passive if they are being used to mask what is really going on in your world. The desire to "be nice" can be inappropriately used as an excuse to not be truthful. True bravery is found in the tension of learning yourself so that you might teach others how to treat you well—actively communicating your needs while being gracious to learn theirs.

Has anyone ever said to you, "Why are you so intense?" or, "You don't have to be such a jerk about it!"? Have you found yourself saying, "Well, I just tell it like it is"? Is it hard for you to listen when someone else is sharing how they feel—do you tend to want to correct every point they make? Have people called you controlling?

People communicating in this style use a fear of not being valuable or heard as fuel to force their way into conversations— demanding their needs be met by cutting other people off, raising their voice and using overbearing body language (intense eyes, hand gestures or close distance). Aggressive communicators tend to react hypercritically to failure and often approach connection without considering the other people involved. This style is prone to rushing into conflict, making sure others know they are wrong and trying to control situations. It is a false attempt to feel powerful by making other people feel powerless.

Aggressive communication is painful because it ultimately pushes other people away. It can quickly break connections by sending the message that the only way to get close is to back down or comply. Aggressive communicators tend to challenge anything that doesn't make sense to them and often do it in a way that is very intimidating to anyone else trying to share vulnerably. Honesty feels like a punch in the gut instead of an invitation into understanding. The need to always be right and say exactly what's on your mind as it comes doesn't leave room for both people in a relationship to feel safe and valuable. This produces cycles of others hiding their feelings, avoiding sharing or fighting back. It doesn't foster safe connection.

Not all aggressive communicators come off as "mean." You can love people and have good intentions while still being driven by a need to control others and situations. Overbearing communication—sending the message, "I always know what's best"—doesn't allow others to feel powerful around you. People can feel smothered or trapped by the need to do things your way. If you want to practice vulnerability, you will have to lay down the "right" to be right. The goal of vulnerability is not to "win or lose" but to stay connected.

AGGRESSIVE

"I MATTER. YOU DON'T."
"IF NO ONE WILL FIGHT FOR ME THEN I MUST FIGHT FOR MYSELF."

ag·gres·sive | \ ə-ˈgre-siv
: tending toward or exhibiting aggression
: marked by combative readiness

PASSIVE-AGGRESSIVE

"YOU TOTALLY MATTER...
NOT REALLY!"
"I'LL FIGHT FOR MYSELF-
BEHIND YOUR BACK!"

pas·sive-ag·gres·sive | \ *pa-siv-ə-'gre-siv*
being, marked by, or displaying behavior characterized by the expression of negative feelings, resentment, and aggression in an unassertive passive way (as through procrastination and stubbornness)

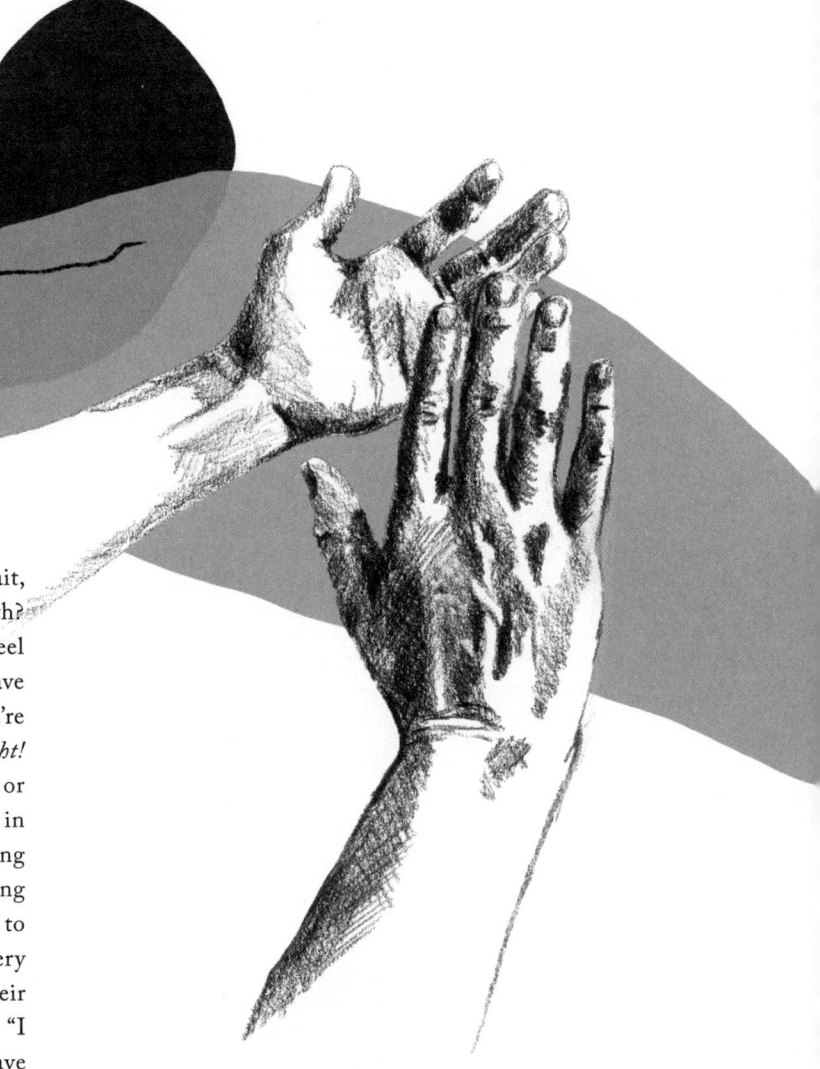

Has anyone ever said to you, "You're so sarcastic!" or, "Wait, what did you say?" as you mutter an annoyance under your breath? Do you prefer to talk to everyone other than the person you feel tension with? "The problem is he never has time for me..." Have you found yourself listening to others and giving cues that you're engaged while inwardly thinking, *This person is a joke!* or, *Yeah right!*

People using this style let the fear of not being valuable or heard justify sabotaging conversations—appearing cooperative in the moment only to sarcastically imply otherwise, saying one thing then doing the complete opposite, rolling their eyes, muttering under their breath and being vague or unclear while trying to find resolve. Passive-aggressive communicators tend to be very judgmental inwardly while externally they only express their judgments in sarcastic comments, jokes or painful questions. "I can't believe you thought that would work." They tend to have very strong opinions but instead of owning their opinions bravely, they hide them in little comments: "I mean if you like that kind of terrible music, good for you!" This style is quick to brush conflict under the rug—no need to "make a big deal" when in fact, things *are* a big deal. It is a false attempt to feel powerful by withholding information only to hurt others with it later.

Passive-aggressive communication is very confusing. It's hard to really know what's expected from you. When they've implied you've "messed up" it feels hurtful because you don't see it coming, like a stab in the back. It creates connections that feel fickle. It sends the message, "I won't tell you what I'm thinking, but you'll feel it." No one is safe and trust is very low. Attempts to connect feel confusing, "I don't want to talk about it—I mean it ruined my night—but it's fine." It's hard to be vulnerable when there is a lack of sincerity and a fear that what you share will only lead to criticism later.

Oftentimes, passive-aggressive communicators resort to manipulation in relationships. The fear of being rejected or misunderstood leads them to "beat around the bush" or talk about people behind their backs. Dropping hints and expecting others to grasp what you are unwilling to acknowledge indicates a lack of trust. The need to feel understood causes passive-aggressive communicators to reach out to the wrong people to help sort through their frustrations. They might do this with the hopes that the person they share with will fight the battle for them or they might do it with the hope of "feeling better." Whatever the reason, the result is not a powerful connection with the person who has actually affected them. It is not healthy to withhold information from the person you're in conflict with in order to appear okay. It actually creates chasms of distance and false peace. True growth comes from ownership and conversation with the right people.

Has anyone ever said to you, "You're really good with people," or, "You know, I'm so glad we had this talk"? Are you able to share your needs and feelings without diminishing someone else's? This is the mark of an assertive lifestyle. It is a mindset that says, "You matter and so do I."

People communicating in this style operate from the truth that they are valuable and worth being heard—taking the necessary time to work through things, practice ownership and clearly communicate what is happening in their world while seeking to understand others. They tend to use inviting body language (clear eye contact, relaxed posture, open hands) and manage to clearly express their needs with confidence. Assertive communicators are not afraid of tension, and instead see it as an opportunity to grow in relational connection. In a conversation, they come ready to listen, a strong advocate for self without getting defensive over disagreement. No matter the circumstance or situation, this style is marked by a willingness to take responsibility and share powerfully without needing to control or convince others. When the Father is the source of your security, it opens up new realms of creativity in how to connect.

Assertive communication is strong and safe—the communicator walks into conversations empowered by worth in the Father's eyes and personal boundaries. If you have decided your tone, topic and goal ahead of time—success is not contingent on the other person's response. This helps take the pressure off of the other person and yourself—*I will be okay no matter your response, but I'd like to invite you into understanding how this affects me.* Sharing becomes a spacious and creative interaction because fear is not the driving force. Assertive communication does not rush—it pauses in tension and re-centers on the goal of understanding. When both people in a conversation feel respected and valuable, vulnerability feels safe and rewarding.

PROMPT: How are you feeling? Can you see how an unhealthy view of yourself or others hinders true vulnerability? Are you having any revelations on why certain relationships have been really hard for you? Awareness is not meant to be a source of shame or resentment—it's meant to help set you free and guide you into responding in love. Stop and let yourself be affected by the information you just read. Can you identify your dominant style of communication? Before moving forward, take a deep breath and pray St. Augustine's prayer, "Grant me, Lord, the wisdom to know myself, that I may know thee."[9]

ASSERTIVE

"I MATTER AND YOU MATTER."
"I AM WORTH FIGHTING FOR AND SO ARE YOU."

as·ser·tive | \ \ ə-ˈsər-tiv
: disposed to or characterized by bold or confident statements and behavior
: having a strong or distinctive flavor or aroma

We all know addressing any level of conflict with success in relationship is not easy. It's often in direct opposition to our cultural normal and a radical departure from the environment we grew up in. So how do we practice a new mindset that says, *You matter and so do I?* In our closest relationships, healthy communication often looks like taking the risk to move toward someone when everything in us wants to move away. It requires that we put down the weapons that we use to defend ourselves and our positions. You have to believe that the way you say things actually does matter and affects their understanding and ability to receive. Other times it looks like moving against the false peace that we are desperate to hide behind, keeping us from the kind of love that Christ calls us to. *What if it's uncomfortable? What if I am misunderstood? What if I lose my likability? What if I am rejected?* It's pressing through an awkward moment and addressing the elephant in the room.

Brave, assertive communication is the result of healthy soul care. We believe that you can't love others more than you love yourself. As we learn to listen and respond to our bodies, our souls and our spirits, we cultivate lives capable of loving well. The healthiest relationships are born of overflow. They are established by a commitment to listening with the goal of understanding. As human beings, we often care more about being heard than hearing, and this is why healthy communication is not automatic to our human experience. Brave communication confronts the hard reality of what we really believe to be true about ourselves, others and God.

The goal in healthy, wholehearted communication is to seek to build a bridge of connection for relationships to flourish, even as people change. Honor and trust are built brick by brick through the practice of brave honesty. It takes courage to be known and seen by another person. It's risky. It takes humility and a soft heart to cultivate the kind of self-awareness that leads me first to the feet of Jesus and then back to the relationship to restore the damage. To share what is going on in my heart means that I must first take the time to take inventory of my own internal world. In our community, we are constantly learning that healthy communication requires our vulnerability and time. Above all, it takes the help of the Holy Spirit. He is the Advocate for mankind to be reconciled, firstly to God and then to one another.

Becoming a healthy communicator is not about a personality type; it is an art that every human must choose to learn. It's a posture, a way you choose to carry yourself in conversation—regardless of how anyone else does. It does this, not out of a sense of superiority, but instead, out of a humility that says, "God has given us both value and He is capable of carrying us through this." In my own life, I have seen that when I act as an advocate and take the time to do the heart work, it brings the most honor to God, myself and the other person. I find myself more likely to respond than react

when things don't go as I had hoped or planned. Taking time to prepare and think through communication is one of the best ways you can honor yourself and another person. Assertive people sow into friendships by caring for their own hearts first, knowing that in doing so, they are making space for Love to have its way.

It takes humility and hard work with the Holy Spirit to become aware of yourself and transform. Remember: You can't love others more than you love yourself. Our desire is that as you grow in self-love rooted in identity in Christ, you would be empowered to love others through healthy communication. In the following pages, you will find the Communication Tool. It has helped our community to practice brave communication in real, everyday life moments. We believe it can help you do the same! We want to charge you to become builders that use this tool to create connection and thriving relationships in your everyday life.

TOOL № 2 : THE COMMUNICATION TOOL

let's talk,

The Communication Tool offers simple guidelines to help you practice vulnerability in your growing relationships; when your feelings get hurt or when a line has been crossed. The quicker you learn to take ownership for yourself—the way you experience pain and cause it—the deeper your relationships will grow. You are not a victim or a picture of perfection. You are human. You are learning and worth the privilege God gave us to practice. When His perfect, steadfast love becomes the source of your confidence, you don't have to control or be controlled by others to find value. To learn His love, you will have to admit you need it. You'll have to practice receiving it in the moments we often try to avoid—failure, risk, mistakes, messy victories. It's seeing His smile in those moments, when you're letting yourself try, that your posture will begin to shift. God didn't just come to save the world, He came to save relationships too. Will you let your patterns of relating to others experience sanctification?

Taking time to think through communication is one of the best ways to honor yourself and the other person. Assertive people sow into friendships by caring for their own hearts first, because they know that is the only way to truly respect another person. Never rush into confrontation, but humble your heart and take the time it requires to stay centered and healthy.

1 WHAT WAS THE MOMENT?

Identify the moment of tension. Include what negatively affected you as well as how you may have negatively affected the other person involved.

Example: Taylor and I made plans to hang out this weekend. When he cancelled last minute AGAIN, I got mad and sent a sarcastic text.

2 COMPLETE AN HONESTY TOOL

Pray, "Holy Spirit, I need your help. What is really going on?"

Take time to complete an Honesty Tool (see pg. 42) about the moment of tension. It's important to begin a Communication Tool having first processed with the Holy Spirit. You want to be connected to His perspective and your heart before practicing any kind of confrontation.

WHAT IS MY TRUST LEVEL WITH THIS PERSON? WHAT IS MY MOTIVE FOR HAVING THIS CONVERSATION?

3

The level of trust and vulnerability you have with the person will affect what you want to clarify and open up about. Do not practice deep vulnerability with a person who hasn't earned it. Next, check your motive. If your motive is still to punish or blame the other person involved, do not move forward. We encourage you to re-read the voice of the Lord and ask for Him to help give you clarity on how to move forward. Remember, the goal is connection.

Example: Taylor and I are good friends. I feel nervous to bring this up, but for us to keep growing in friendship, I think that a conversation would help us to build trust. I want him to be able to be honest with me about what's going on, but I don't want this to keep happening.

4

WHAT DO I NEED TO ADDRESS AND OWN?

Identify what affected you. Remember what you're addressing should be situation specific. Don't dig up old pain to make an impact. Identify what you need to own or apologize for.

-I feel hurt that Taylor keeps canceling plans with me.
-This keeps happening and I want to know if something is going on.
-I want to own and apologize for where I was rude and sarcastic via text.
-Moving forward, I want to be honest instead of sarcastically implying how I feel.

5

HOW DO I WANT TO COMMUNICATE THIS?

Write a practice script for what you'd like to share. Keep it short and simple. Be sure to ask questions that allow space for them to respond. Once you're done, read over your script and remove words and phrases that may provoke a defensive response. Remember, you're not addressing every issue in your relationship, you're using this moment to build a bridge of trust.

Taylor, could we talk about what happened with our plans this weekend? First, I want to apologize for sending that sarcastic text. Will you forgive me? (Pause) Can we talk a little more about what is going on? (Pause) When I got your text about needing to cancel our plans, I felt frustrated. This has happened a few times now and I'm starting to wonder if you really want to spend time with me. Is there something going on that I don't know about? You matter to me and I really want to grow in my ability to talk openly. I don't want sarcasm to be the way I communicate my frustration. I recognize that sometimes things come up, but I'd like to be able to make plans and stick to them. Is that something that you are willing to do?

TOOL Nº 2 : THE COMMUNICATION TOOL

here's my example,

by JESSIE MILLER

THE MOMENT: Co-worker at school repeatedly asking me to start her class

Have you ever felt like a co-worker was taking advantage of you? As a teacher, every one of my school days began with a planning block. Ninety minutes of me and Jesus planning and prepping for the day ahead over my cup of coffee. This was my time—a crucial, sacred part of my daily routine. One morning I noticed the new teacher's students were still lined up outside her classroom door when the bell rang, so I decided to let them in for her.

I stayed with them, helping start the day, until she arrived. "Aw, thank you so much!" she exclaimed as she rushed in the door late. "Sure! No problem, glad to help," I responded. But then, a couple days later, it happened again, and *again*. I started getting frequent phone calls, "Hey, Mrs. Miller. I'm running late and I'm going to need you to open my door." I felt the frustration rising. *Now she's just using me!* But I continued to unlock her classroom door morning after morning and supervise her students—sure she would eventually sense my frustration.

What started as a genuine desire to help turned into being taken advantage of. I was getting progressively more upset. My subtle hints weren't working and after about a month of this happening at least once a week, I was done being nice. I was agitated. I wanted to avoid her and I found myself thinking judgmental thoughts. *Who does she think she is, talking to me like this?* I knew I was triggered and ready for an honest conversation with Jesus.

1 WHAT WAS THE MOMENT?

My co-worker keeps asking me to start her class — and now she's not asking, she's telling me!

2. COMPLETE AN HONESTY TOOL

1. Stop and ask the Holy Spirit for help.

   Holy Spirit, what's going on? Why is this situation with my co-worker pressing me so much?

2. Get honest with how you're feeling.

   God, I feel used. I'm upset that she doesn't seem to be considering how her requests are affecting me. I was just trying to do the good Christian thing and love well and now I feel like I'm paying for it. Why can't you make her see the ways I am letting her know I don't want to help anymore? It feels like you aren't fighting for me. Why do I notice the messages everyone sends, but no one notices mine? Why do I have to do everything?

3. Reflect and Exchange. *Are there any lies I am believing?* Exchange these lies for truth.

   I am used. I am punished. I am a failure. God isn't helping me. God is asking too much of me.

4. Listen to God's voice. Journal His response.

   Jessie, your heart to help is so beautiful to me. Your willingness to give and see opportunity in the midst of negativity is brilliant. But, you are not stuck in a mission I doomed you to. I am not withholding my help — I am simply offering it in a way that will bear more fruit in your life. I want to walk through this tension with you. I want you to use your voice and try the very thing you are most afraid of — sharing the truth. My love has come to set you free, not from tension, but from the lies that warp your view of the circumstances that surround you. Jessie, love can say yes and love can say no. It's not all or nothing. You are aware of your need for a boundary now and it is my joy to help you find a way to communicate in love. You are capable. It's time to practice the full range of love.

3. WHAT IS MY TRUST LEVEL WITH THIS PERSON? WHAT IS MY MOTIVE FOR HAVING THIS CONVERSATION?

We are co-workers and our trust level is low. I only see her at school, she isn't involved in several areas of my life. I feel where this is affecting how I see her. I don't want to stay angry about something I haven't addressed. I want to practice drawing a new boundary. I hope it will improve our working dynamic.

4. WHAT DO I NEED TO ADDRESS AND OWN?

- My planning block is important to my day.
- I need to feel like my time is respected.
- I would like her to approach me with a different tone.
- I am willing to help, but need the option to say yes or no.
- I want to own that I could have brought this up sooner.
- I am sorry for waiting this long to talk to you about it.

WHAT DO I NEED TO COMMUNICATE?

Could we talk about you asking me to help start your class on the days you're running late? My planning block is really important to me and I rely on that time to get ready for the day. When you call last minute and say, "I'm running late, I'm going to need you to open my door today," it feels like you are telling me what to do and not considering my own responsibilities. This feels especially true when you end up actually needing me to watch your students. Does that make sense? I want to apologize for not bringing this up sooner. I want to own that I didn't have to wait this long. Will you forgive me? I want us to feel like we can help each other, but I need to feel respected in the way you ask and presented with an opportunity to say no without putting your students in jeopardy. It would help me if you could reach out to other teachers as well when you need class coverage. I care about you and believe we can find ways of helping that work for both of us.

how it actually went

Let's be honest, I was so nervous—borderline terrified. I had never talked to a co-worker about something like this and it felt like a big deal. I didn't know how she would take it and felt the pressure to do it perfectly. But, I had a plan and the Holy Spirit. I kept reminding myself that this conversation was a step in the right direction, but it didn't have to fix everything. We were both worth pressing through the tension of a conversation. At lunch, I asked if she had time to talk with me after school. She seemed a little caught off guard, but agreed.

Our conversation went better than I imagined. At first, she felt defensive, but the Holy Spirit highlighted her own fear of getting "walked over." He helped me stay centered. I didn't punish her, listing all the times I had felt bullied by her. Instead, I owned my part and redrew the new boundary; sharing from what I had crafted with the Father. When talking about what would help me feel respected, I told her that the phrase and tone of, "I'm going to need you to…" on the phone felt like a disrespectful command. She apologized immediately and was genuinely shocked, "I never meant to tell you what to do or disrespect you. In my family 'I'm going to need you to…' is considered a way of asking a question." She agreed to work on phrasing her requests as a question ("Would you…"), leaving me space to say no. All in all, we talked about ten minutes and in that time connection was restored.

I mattered. My help was valuable and worth boundaries that were consistent with my capacity. She mattered. She didn't need to be "put in her place"; she was worth the conversation about what messages she was sending me and the opportunity to grow as I shared what I needed her to change. In the end, we both felt more valued by the other, and it opened the door for more conversations as we continued working together.

The momentum of connection is directly related to what we're willing to risk on vulnerability.
— A.R. Sampson

35mm film photography by NIC FARLEY

THE FRIEND - LEADER

DYNAMIC

an interview with MELISSA HELSER and JUSTINA STEVENS

by ALLIE SAMPSON
photography from personal collections

I've seen the two of them like this a thousand times before—relaxed into the couch, coffee mugs in hand, making easy conversation and laughing at each other's jokes. When people encounter Justina and Melissa together, they immediately feel the depth of their friendship. These women have spent over a decade working closely alongside one another building trust, celebrating milestones, choosing to be vulnerable, pressing through conflict and forging a connection that's both genuine and inspiring. Being around them is like sitting by a fireplace: effortless, warm and inviting.

Justina Stevens serves on Jonathan and Melissa's Core Leadership Team and has helped pioneer the Cageless Birds collective and The 18 Inch Journey schools for the last thirteen years. She is the Art Director for the Cageless Birds, where she oversees all of our handmade goods and visual arts departments alongside Melissa, making a space for creatives to be connected to our mission while creating excellent work. She developed a visual journaling curriculum for our 18 Inch Journey schools, which has become a fundamental rhythm of our community. Justina is an essential part of the Cageless Birds team and has given over a decade to discipling a generation into wholeness.

One of the most common questions Justina and Melissa get asked is about their friendship and how they navigate carrying a mission together while also walking out a friend-leader dynamic. I sat down with Justina and Melissa to ask them questions about how they've walked out their multi-faceted friendship.

WHEN DID YOUR STORIES FIRST CONNECT?

J: Well…I was ten!

M: Justina was young. I was good friends with her older sister, Candace. I really got to watch Justina grow up while I was growing up too. Jonathan and I were in our twenties, freshly married.

J: You were super cool and you were dating the cool worship leader! I think the first time I came to A Place for the Heart, I was eleven and it was for your wedding. I just remember thinking, "Wow! I'm at Jonathan and Melissa's wedding!"

M: Initially it was an acquaintanceship, but then Justina came to our camp when she was a teenager. That's what Jonathan and I really pressed into in our twenties—we called them creative worship camps. Our heart was to give teenagers more than an experience—we wanted to really teach them to spend time with the Lord. Justina came to our camps for years. She had this big hair and was super artsy, and we fell in love with her.

HOW DID YOU STAY CONNECTED THROUGHOUT THE YEARS?

J: You and Jonathan have always been those wonderfully bizarre people who would go spend the night at someone's college dorm. Yes, Melissa did that! Multiple times, she came to see my art, watch my dance performances, sit in coffee shops and speak into my life. Now in my thirties I'm like, *Nobody does that!* There was that divine connection. But it's also because you and Jonathan decided you were going to be lovers of people. I mean, that's special, for someone with small children to love like that. Even when people ask me: "You've been running with the Helsers for so long; is there anything else you want to do?" I'm like, "No, because I've fallen in love with loving."

M: I think it's important for leaders to pay attention to that feeling of: *I want to go the distance for this person… drive three hours to see if they're okay, sit with them when they break up with their boyfriend and listen to them.* I was really sick during that time, but there was this beautiful desire and this connection of care and love. I think it was that consistency—of going to visit her, asking her questions, giving her time and space to process—that progressed into Justina coming back to serve our camps and schools every summer throughout college. Eventually, she joined our community full-time.

HOW DID YOU LEARN TO WORK AND CARRY A MISSION TOGETHER? WHAT MAKES FOR A SUCCESSFUL WORKING FRIENDSHIP?

J: We've done a lot of projects together. We have schools six months out of the year and in the other six months we pursue all sorts of creative endeavors: *Cultivate*, worship, all of our amazing small businesses. There's a bond that happens when you commit to a project—like us sowing seven years into our community's devotional, *Cultivate*. That first volume, we literally designed in Cadence's room, working late into the night and laughing hysterically. There were so many days during that project where I was moody and a total stinker! In those moments, I needed correction from my leader, but I also needed help from my friend, all while working on a deadline with my boss. In those times, Melissa always chose my heart first. She discipled me in the moment and gave me feedback. She put healthy pressure on me to grow and she pointed me to Jesus. So many of those projects really shaped our dynamic. They helped me mature and they created a platform for us to grow a lot of trust. Now I find myself in many moments with our staff when they're hitting the same walls that I hit with Melissa, and I smile and think, *Really good fruit is going to come from this!*

M: The refreshing thing for us has been moving in and out of that discipleship-work balance. Just when we get tired in our season of doing schools, it shifts, and we focus on pioneering creative projects and discipling our team. Our friendship is never void of that element of discipleship. Our value system is people-forward and people first. The dynamic of having a work relationship actually brought a level of practical, logical, everyday tension to our relationship that was really good for us. It's that tension of: "Okay we're showing up, neither of us are in a good mood and we have people looking to us for leadership." I think it's been really healthy. For us, the projects, the dreaming, the risk-factors have all been opportunities to build trust.

ARE YOU IN EACH OTHER'S INNER CIRCLE? WHAT DID IT TAKE TO ESTABLISH THAT KIND OF TRUST?

M: For sure. Six months ago, I came to work in a terrible mood and I was ranting about something. Justina just looked at me and said, "Mel, what is going on?" "Nothing is going on. Let's just get this done." "What is going on?" I love that I've given her permission to ask me that kind of question. Of course, I broke down sobbing. Not everyone I lead has permission to ask that. I'm not suggesting that you give the most vulnerable parts of your heart to everyone you lead. But the reward of creating a strong team is that you can bring both your beauty and your chaos to the table.

Besides Jonathan, there's nobody in the world I've built more trust with than Justina. Our friendship holds a lot of dynamics: boss, friend, leader…and Justina and I have gotten really good at changing those hats. If there's a moment in the middle of the workday when I'm in a lot of pain and I really need "friend Justina," she knows, because we've committed to growing in trust together. I'd also say that nobody can make Jonathan and I laugh like Justina. In our dynamic, there's a lot of space to be ourselves. She's been in the room for so many moments when Jonathan and I are being really goofy, or having an argument or making mistakes, and she's there for it. I love that a lot of our core staff have been in those moments with us, and that we gave them space to really see us.

We don't do that with everyone. When I say "inner circle," I'm not meaning this really pretentious group. But I do think everyone has an inner circle whether they know it or not. It's really valuable to know who you can trust and who you are committed to walking with long-term. I see that in the life of Jesus. He knew His three. He was so committed to them and vulnerable with them. He begged them to stay awake with Him. In the same way, there is a circle of vulnerability that is surrounding my and Jonathan's marriage. Because at the end of the day, it's got to be the people we trust deeply that we let into our lives—there has to be a currency of trust.

WHAT'S IT LIKE FOR ONE OF YOUR LEADERS TO ALSO BE ONE OF YOUR CLOSEST FRIENDS?

J: I've appreciated having a friend who is ahead of me. Receiving that gift completely from the Lord has looked like purging my idea of arrival. I used to think, *Maybe…in a couple years…I'll be the friend that will have the perfect advice for Melissa!* But that's such a shallow version of what friendship is. When you're wrestling with the idea of arrival, you miss out on so much of the beauty of the friend-leader dynamic.

I specifically remember, maybe three or four years ago, sitting with you and vocalizing that frustration: "I just feel like I can't be the friend you need. I want to be the friend that gives you advice." And you looked at me and said, "That's not what I need from you." I just started crying and felt so much relief, realizing that it had all been a misconception. You told me, "All I need is for you to show up with your whole heart." That was so liberating. If you're not having those kinds of conversations in the friend-leader dynamic, I think it's impossible. Checking expectations often has been the only way. In the friend-leader dynamic, it's easy to make up worlds in your mind that you just have to talk about. Because most of the time they're not real. I think that's a huge key to community and to the friend-leader role.

Even when I think about the girls I'm leading now, this understanding has landed in my heart. I never once think, *I just wish they'd grow up and get on my level.* That's not a natural thought for me. I look on their seasons of life and think, *Gosh, that was hard. That is real, I can remember that moment in my life, and I want to help save you time.* That same feeling is what I've received from Melissa.

YOU'VE WALKED WITH EACH OTHER THROUGH A LOT OF SEASONS AND STORMS. DO YOU HAVE ANY KEYS FOR HOW TO NAVIGATE DIFFERENT SEASONS?

M: Ten years ago, emotional health really became a part of our discipleship school. It revolutionized the way we did leadership, ministry and friendships. Emotional health was a game-changer for us. It gave us keys and language in the midst of being creative, highly emotional people. Emotional health—like processing with God, practicing vulnerability, communication, conflict resolution—has kept us from performing for each other. It's helped us understand our internal worlds and stay honest with each other. Justina is thirty-two. I'm forty now. I can't even imagine being where Justina is emotionally and spiritually when I was thirty-two. We've experienced sadness, joy, tragedy, loss—the whole gambit of what makes a friendship real and true. And the emotional health part of that—not just tools, but the commitment to learn tools together—has been one of the most beautiful, maturing parts of my friendship with Justina. Which leads to that moment where, besides Jonathan, no one can read me like her.

WHAT WOULD YOU SAY TO PEOPLE WHO WANT TO HAVE A HEALTHY FRIEND-LEADER DYNAMIC BUT DON'T KNOW WHERE TO START?

M: I think you just start with the one the Holy Spirit is drawing you to. Inviting one person into your culture, into your family. And respecting that they have something to offer. I think that from the beginning, Justina felt respected by Jonathan and trying to give them advice for the fiftieth time. However, it's these small steps that are teaching us to reach for that love that never runs dry—that love that we access in the Father's heart. That's where we are growing authority. If you're wondering how to get started, stop looking for the ideal, because that's not how you grow in authority or love.

M: I totally agree. People often say to me, "I just wish this person I'm leading would be more like…" I think that's idealism. *If I had the ideal team, or the ideal people to lead, then it would just be easy and there'd be no mess.* I think people think that's the case when they look in on our community, but it couldn't be further from the truth. It's like Proverbs 14:4, where it pretty much says, "If there's no mess in the stall there's no harvest…" If you want it pristine and clean and ideal and you want it to look Instagram-worthy, then you

  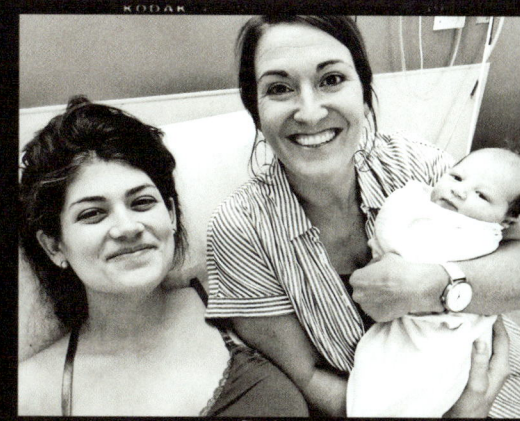

me. We knew she had something valuable to offer and that she played an important role in what we were dreaming into. Jonathan and I have such a specific kind of community. A lot of people don't have that, but they have their table, where they can build belonging. More than anything, it's just asking the Lord for creative ideas. Start with investing in one person. Ask the Lord for a clear invitation to who you could love and pour into. For us, it was never about what we could gain from Justina. Jonathan and I were just so drawn to her and loved her so much. And now her friendship is one of the greatest treasures of my life.

J: One thing I've observed is that neither you or Jonathan have looked for the ideal setting. You've looked for where you can love, and you've consistently made space for love. I watched you access the love of God for me, and for so many other people when it was extraordinarily inconvenient. And now when the world looks in on our little community, it looks ideal—which it's not—but it looks that way because of all the tiny steps we've made where we reached for love, and love is attractive. There's nothing ideal about feeling exhausted at the end of the day and my husband and I opening our home to a young dating couple, actually don't get a harvest. To have a harvest of discipleship like Jesus is to embrace the reality that there's just going to be mess. We'd be lying to say there wasn't mess. More than anything, our desire is to give people the hope that they can do it the way Jesus did it. He didn't pick the ideal people, and they ended up turning the whole world upside down because they felt the love in His eyes. They felt the rebuke, the correction, the extravagance, the joy, the laughter. They felt true friendship.

I think also, if you want a powerful friend-leader relationship, you have to practice vulnerability. It's the only way to build authority and create a deep and lasting friendship. I think that would be my challenge to anyone in leadership: Who are you getting vulnerable with? Even if they're younger than you. Vulnerability is to share your need. It's to say, "Will you pray for me? Will you help? I'm feeling overwhelmed." If a friendship has no conflict, then it's not growing. That's been a huge key. *We're growing together and I'm committed to you. I'm committed to saying I'm sorry, to being wrong, to asking for help even if you don't know how to help me.* I'm committed to being vulnerable with those who are closest to my heart.

JOYFUL

I love to get things done. At A Place for the Heart, I wear many hats but my main roles are leading the kitchen and managing the grounds. My job is to get things done and done on time, whether it's putting a three-course meal on the table for a school's opening dinner, or painting a new cabin in the sweat of the Carolina summer heat. Like in most homes, our kitchen is a hub of activity. In a normal week, we prepare around 400 meals, and in the two months of our largest discipleship school, more than 17,000 meals are served. While these numbers convey the magnitude of food we are preparing, they mean absolutely nothing to me if our meals aren't cooked and served in a space where connection is the top priority. When Jesus summed up the greatest commandment—love God, love people—He made connection our highest calling. This value should affect every part of our lives, including the workplace. Every day there are chances to fall behind in schedule, get anxious or become fixated on the task and forget to care for each other. If, while getting dinner on the table, we stress ourselves out, speak sharply or use anxiety as a motivator, we haven't done our job well. So even when the pressure is on, I have committed myself to disengaging anxiety and staying at peace in the workplace. This hasn't come naturally; it's something that I've had to learn.

Anxiety can be so incredibly common at work. We all know that feeling of deadlines pressing, details crowding, stress climbing. Problems and mistakes are inevitable, and in response, anxiety urges us to make brash decisions and tensely interact with others. Instead of being led by anxiety, I've learned to pause, step back from the task and acknowledge my heart and the hearts of those around me. A few years ago, I hit some major anxiety while I was leading a team in painting a new cabin. We were on a short deadline, and without realizing it, we'd used two completely different types of paint. When I saw that there were patches of matte and semi-gloss paint all over the walls, my stomach dropped. My mind started teeming with thoughts: *I cannot believe this happened. We don't have time for this! Did I really mess up this bad?* It was already late in the day; my team was tired. My boss and co-manager were both away on a trip; I was alone with the responsibility to fix it. Plus we were days from new students moving in. So, I took a deep breath. I was very conscious of how I responded; I knew that my team would follow my response. If I freaked out, they would all freak out. If I reacted with anxiety, it would send them into a tailspin. I spoke calmly, "Guys, I think we had a mix-up with the paint. I'm going to need a few minutes. Can everyone take a dinner break?"

Next, I addressed my own anxiety. I found a close friend and asked to externally process with her, vocalizing my shame and embarrassment. A moment of vulnerability was key—it defused the pressure I felt and helped me recognize what was fueling my anxiousness: the belief that I was a total failure. It only took a few minutes to repent.

Then I asked the Father for wisdom and made an alternative plan with clarity and peace. When I returned to my team, I invited them into that same peace. Practicing an appropriate amount of vulnerability with those you lead can be beautiful—vulnerability that doesn't make your team responsible to take care of you, but that brings connection and unity. I let my team into my process: I was honest about the fact that the setback was a bummer, that it wasn't anyone's fault and that I had disengaged stress and we could all do the same. I also charged them to stay in peace, but to keep up the pace to make up for lost time. It's possible to work quickly and efficiently from a place of joy. All of this—from catching the mistake, to releasing anxiety, to empowering my team—took about fifteen minutes. Mistakes are real, and so are deadlines, but it's worth it to pause and choose peace. When we work in a way that reflects God's nature, it keeps us connected in the value of honoring each other's hearts, and it always glorifies Him.

I'm continually presented with these same choices—whether or not to walk in peace; whether or not to see others in the midst of task—not only during large-scale projects, but also in everyday moments. As I've practiced making these choices over the last decade, I've learned a few more keys along the way that I'd love to share:

WORK

by MARTHA McRAE
photography by MORGAN CAMPBELL

CONNECT

Practicing connection communicates to those you lead that the task never outweighs the importance of their hearts. Connection helps us feel secure in our unity, individually valued and ready to work together when the pressure of "crunch time" comes. At the beginning of a task, these are things I'm sure to do:
• Look everyone in the eyes, to personally acknowledge each member of the team.
• Pray together, which connects us to the affection of the Father and helps us receive His perspective.
• Offer up a question to everyone in the middle of a project; I ask them about their day, what they did in other departments or what the Father has been teaching them.

COMMUNICATE

How we speak to each other can be the difference between an environment of peace or one of friction and division. There isn't a single staff member who I haven't pulled aside at some point to check in with them after they've communicated poorly. And there've been plenty of moments when I've apologized for something I've said or for my tone of voice when giving instruction. Here are some keys for communicating with my team:
• I aim for clarity and kindness in my communication, whether I'm delegating tasks or correcting a mistake.
• Every day I talk through the day's goal with the entire team. It's much easier to move from one element of a task to another if everyone understands the scope of our plan. It also eliminates room for assumption, and it helps us remain flexible when timing changes (which it does, all the time).
• I remind everyone of our value: we honor each other in every moment of the day and if we miss the mark, we re-center and apologize. Our apologies are not a courtesy, but a recognition: *I've stepped outside of what keeps the team safe and affected my teammates.* We've created a culture where it is safe to acknowledge mistakes and failures and then adjust our behavior.

INCENTIVE

When a timeline requires quick execution, it's better to be motivated by incentive rather than fear. When we're running late in a task, we have the option of lingering in thoughts like, *If I don't get this done, I've failed. Everyone will know I'm a fraud. My job is going to be on the line.* But negative self-talk is a sign that we've lost connection with the Holy Spirit. Instead, I like to encourage work with incentive. Here are some ideas from my experience to motivate your team:
• I'll say to my team, "Let's press in and get this done so we can all take a break and grab a cold drink!"
• Or I might say, "If we get into go-mode now, we can finish on time and get plenty of rest tonight!"

PROMPT:
I do love getting things done. Keeping peace and connection at the center of demanding work isn't easy; it's a choice I have to make every day. But in our workplace, our friendships have grown stronger, our communication more confident and our hearts kinder. Whether we are sitting at God's feet in worship and adoration like Mary, or carrying out a task like Martha, we can choose to do all with love, prioritizing the value of connection with Jesus and each other.

In what scenarios are you rushing past connection to get a task done? Has task become more important to you than people? Take time to reflect. Then pray, "Holy Spirit, I repent for putting efficiency above connection, and for overlooking the people you've put in my life. I ask for the sensitivity to re-engage people as the most valuable part of any task. In Jesus' name, amen."

telephone

by PHYLLIS UNKEFER

I. Telephone

There are wires
strung between poles
from here to anywhere.
A black spiderweb
swaying above cities,
catching nothing but sound.

We once tilted telephones
to our shoulders
and didn't think a thing
of how sleekly our voices
could swim along wires,
how quickly words could
bloom in our ears,
how our evening
murmurings feathered into hearing
from a hundred miles away.

Any time of day,
we spun phone cords in our fingers
as the receiver siphoned
a crackling *happy birthday*,
a hummed *how are you?*,
or that payphone plea
for a ride home.

It was the first place we learned to
speak to the unknown.
Each time, a blind hello.

If you, by chance,
studied the telephone lines,
you'd see them slightly swell,
steeped with a stream
of our questions,
our laughters, our edged silences.
Our *hello's?, are you there's?,*
when are you coming home's?
The dipping, brimming,
tightening of our tone.
They know the searching
of our voices for listening ears.
And they sway above our sidewalks
crisscrossing the air,
waiting for that pause,
that momentary stillness,
that slow, deep breath
of being heard.

II. Cellular Phone

But now, it's a matter of flight.
A cell phone is a glorified system
of paper airplanes
hurled invisibly through space
that surpass oceans and
state-lines and unopened doors
from inside the pocket of your coat.

Our voices fly.
Airborne conversations carve the air,
headed to God knows where.
Around us, phone calls roam,
zigzag, spin past,
with which we unwittingly collide.
Have you felt it?
That splash of feeling?
That sudden emotion that drifts in
when you're sweeping the floor
or mid-step on the stairs?
It's talk gliding midair.
A phone call, on course, that soars
all the way through you.
Till her firecracker laughter,
or his confused pause,
or that breeze of shy secrets
from their lightly unfolding hearts
brush against your bones
and for a second,
you're not sure where you are.

Voices surround us.
Waves of them crash toward the sky,
and one of them is mine.
It's gone beyond me.
It's outrun my feet.
My voice has landed
where I've never touched the ground:
Malawi, Peru,
to a muffled operator in Qatar,
and to you; three states away,
elbow on kitchen table,
rinsed in morning light.
My voice is in flight.
Swimming through desert
to find you,
slipping past mountains,
wrinkling static
and smoothing back out
to deliver the only words I have.

To tie us like a string
between windows
and paper cups and this
many years of trust.
To insist that distance
is just another sea
that's willing to part
between you and I
if you don't mind
folding these paper airplanes,
floating them on this wind
and pausing slow and
long enough to hear.

PAST SOCIAL PROTOCOL

ON CREATING DOORWAYS
FOR GOD TO WALK THROUGH

by STEPHEN ROACH

JESUS WAS OFTEN ACCUSED BY THE RELIGIOUS LEADERS OF HIS DAY FOR HANGING OUT WITH ALL THE WRONG PEOPLE. HE BROKE SOCIAL PROTOCOL AND SAT AT THE TABLE WITH "TAX COLLECTORS" AND "SINNERS."

He attended dinner parties and wedding celebrations; He stayed at the homes of those who did not follow Jewish Law. The Gospels give us numerous examples of Jesus welcoming women, non-Jewish followers and outcasts of society into His inner circle. In Mark 2:17 (NKJV), Jesus responds to His accusers by saying, "Those who are well have no need of a physician, but those who are sick. I did not come to call the righteous, but sinners, to repentance."

In my own life I have come to value friendships with people of other perspectives and persuasions than my own. This is not for the sake of converting them, but to receive the gift of the other. Some of my atheist friends have built my faith in ways I would have never known had I chosen to live an insular life only among those who think and believe the same as myself. In the same way, I have found sharing my faith in Jesus produces much richer fruit when he or she feels valued, has been given a seat at the table and isn't treated as a project.

My music and art in particular have long served as catalysts for building bridges into the lives of those I wouldn't likely see on a Sunday morning. I recall in the early days of my music group, Songs of Water, we toured and performed everywhere from folk festivals to new age environments, nightclubs and even a few Cowboy churches in Texas. I recall several encounters with people who responded by saying, "Your music healed my heart," or, "There is a peace and a presence in your music I haven't experienced before." Often this led to opportunities for sharing the meaning behind the music. Friendships were built, and we cultivated the relational equity needed to speak to the deeper issues of a person's life.

In much the same way, not all of the guests I interview for the *Makers & Mystics* podcast share the same faith practice as my own. I recall one artist in particular who described herself to me as a "retired Christian." I was surprised when she agreed to do the interview as much of the podcast's content is explicitly Christian in nature. At first, she was a bit nervous, I suppose suspecting I would ask about her faith; but as the interview progressed, she relaxed and opened up on her own about her background: "You know, I grew up Southern Baptist," she said. "Really? Wow! Tell me more about that," I responded. "Yeah, I even went to seminary and studied theology." "What happened?" She confided in me how the problem of evil had shipwrecked her faith: "I haven't spoken to anyone about these things in years and never publicly." The experience of her being valued and accepted by a person of faith without any further expectation opened a door for her to begin working through years of hurt and disappointment concerning the Church. I'll never know the fullness of how this moment impacted her, but I know I created a doorway for God to walk in and heal what only He could.

This is the beautiful invitation we have been given as artists of faith. Jesus has shown us His example of loving the unloved, of going past social protocol and giving a seat at the table to those He desires to encounter. The story of Zacchaeus describes this wonderfully: "Zacchaeus, make haste and come down, for today I must stay at your house" (Luke 19:5, NKJV). Zacchaeus, whose name meant pure but was known for being impure, hurried down the tree in response to Jesus. He began spouting his credentials of how he gave half his income to the poor and restored over and above anything he took from others. But Jesus never asked him to qualify himself. Jesus received him before he had done anything to prove himself worthy. Meanwhile, the Pharisees complained because Jesus had "gone to be a guest with a man who is a sinner." The Son of God reminded them that Zacchaeus, too, was a son of Abraham and that He had come to seek and to save that which is lost. Jesus' acceptance of Zacchaeus led to an immediate transformation and gave him the opportunity to become what his name implied. Pure.

PROMPT: In the upcoming days, pray and ask God to help you build a bridge into the world outside of the Church. Jesus knew how to speak a language everyone understood. His stories and parables reached the religious and unreligious alike. Ask God to give you a language to connect with those outside the community of faith.

LET'S TALK ABOUT MY

MI—ST—AK—ES

photography by
MORGAN CAMPBELL

Intro by
JUSTINA STEVENS

The Cageless Birds lead internships for a handful of our 18 Inch Journey school alumni every year. The eleven month commitment is an intentional time of pouring into several different departments on our land: assisting leather craft or pottery, serving in grounds maintenance and helping run our retreats, camps and schools. Each intern joins the community and intentionally pursues wholeness by cultivating emotional health through practicing the Honesty Tool, working out healthy communication and receiving feedback from managers and leaders.

Without fail, this season is life changing. Many of them hit their biggest walls through circumstances that arise during their work on the land, and the Father always uses it for their good, their growth and their transformation. The following three writings are by our current staff members who have looked back on their internships years ago and can see specific moments of tension that changed them forever. Our desire is for you to feel a wave of inspiration and joy as you see how the Father uses failure, tension and mistakes to create brand new, healthy beliefs in any willing heart.

WHEN SHAME DR—IV—ES

Keys to Overcoming Shame

BY CADE GARLOCK

SMASH! I am frozen in fear. *I'm such an idiot. This isn't happening...THIS ISN'T HAPPENING!* I've just crashed the back of a big ol' Toyota Tundra—and this isn't just any truck, but my manager Martha McRae's beloved truck. I haven't just made a small scratch or dent; I have warped the truck bed to the point where the tailgate won't open. In my mind, mistakes, especially the monumental ones, are unacceptable. So, I pause and prepare myself for the yelling that was sure to ensue. I walk into the kitchen where Martha is sitting at the counter, prepping some s'mores for our retreat guests. "Martha?" I say through trembling teeth, "Something bad happened. I was backing your truck up the driveway, and I couldn't really see…I crashed the back of your truck into the wall. I am so sorry. So, so, so sorry..." My clammy hands were shaking and I felt sick to my stomach. In the few seconds of silence between us, I felt the all-too-familiar feeling: Shame. *I can't believe I let this happen.*

Martha sat there for a moment with a serious but compassionate look in her eyes. She took a breath; I could tell that she had heard the crash sound and had decided not to rush out. She locked eyes with me and calmly said, "I forgive you, Cade. We're going to need to finish our day—our guests are waiting, but let's reconnect tonight and talk this through." I felt shocked and confused. I wanted her to yell at me. But there was Martha, peacefully communicating the next tasks to the team, not avoiding eye contact with me, not punishing me, but making space for both of us to process and complete our task.

Later that evening, after our retreat guests headed to their cabins, Martha and I got to talk. We walked back out to the driveway to inspect the truck. To my utter shock she spoke very kindly, almost with amusement in her voice, "Now *that's* a dent! Well, accidents happen. We will get ahold of the insurance company and see what we can do. It's okay, Cade. It's just a truck." I was visibly pale from the shock of the situation. I had no words and honestly I was still shaking. She promptly turned around to walk back in the kitchen. I stood there with my mouth wide open. *That's it? She's got to be pretending. She has to be fuming. I need to be punished.* I had already made up my mind that if Martha wasn't going to shame me, then I would shame myself. That was right, that was fair.

Martha looked up and saw me, and I mean *really* saw me. "Accidents happen and the truck can be fixed, Cade, but your heart is the important thing at stake. I can see that you're not okay. It seems like you're beating yourself up, and I just don't think that's necessary." She saw right through me, and she walked me through the truth that grace covers me completely—not just in my good moments, but in the bad ones, too. Martha spoke with kindness and strength, telling me it was time for me to carve a new path in the woods of my heart. It was time to let the road of shame crumble and instead build a new road, one that leads to the Trinity no matter the situation.

Shame gives you cloudy perspective and causes you to forget the bulletproof truth that every part of you is loved. It will separate you from all relationships and you will eventually end up in an isolated prison where insults are your only cellmates. Shame says that you are a mistake. But praise God, there is a better way. This moment with Martha turned into an extremely life-altering situation. One where God stepped in, put His stake in the ground and declared, "It's time for a change!" One that looked like believing that mistakes are a walkway for connection and honesty and healing. The reality that He can take my mess-ups and turn them into good has transformed the way I see and empowered me to stand up to the voice of shame that comes to diminish me when I make mistakes.

Keys to Becoming Powerful
BY HANNAH HAYWORTH

WHEN YOU GO AG—AIN—ST THE GRAIN

"Hey Hannah! I'm so glad you came in here! We were just talking about the event this weekend and I worked out all the details so that you can have your birthday off! Happy birthday!!" I was crushed. My manager had no idea, but I had been looking forward to working this event for weeks. We were going to be setting up a merch table at a local worship night, and I was excited to spend the day with some of my best friends, running the booth and meeting people who loved our ministry. She might as well have said, "I'm ruining your birthday, and I'm doing it last minute."

Disappointment consumed me. "Oh…okay great…yeah that's fine. Thanks for telling me." I started shutting down, and she caught it right away. "Hannah, what's going on?" Suddenly I became hyper-aware of everyone else in the room. I didn't know what was going on, and I began to interrogate myself. *Why am I so emotional about this? I'm acting like a child.* She was clearly confused and asked: "Do you really want to work on your birthday?" I froze up. "I'm not trying to take something away from you." My manager began openly addressing a pattern she'd noticed of my struggle to receive. She was calling me out in front of everyone in the room. I tried to listen, but struggled to hear her over my own embarrassment. I caught fragmented sentences in between panicked thoughts. *Who is watching? I'm exposed. I didn't even realize this about myself and now it's on display for everyone to see. Why do we have to do this here?* I listened as best I could, made eye contact between tears, scrambled to apologize and got out as fast as possible.

For some context, I have a strong tendency toward passivity, especially when it comes to interactions with leaders. Conflict has caught me in a "You're right, I'm wrong" mentality. For years, I associated respecting authority with immediate compliance. I thought that respect looked like always saying yes, keeping quiet and quickly doing whatever was asked of me. Later that night, I did an Honesty Tool (see pg. 42) and the Lord showed me that what I was feeling was valid. I had been embarrassed in front of a group of people, and trust with my manager had been broken. He challenged me to speak up—to own what I was feeling and share with my boss how she had affected me. I was nervous, but I knew that if I followed through, trust could be rebuilt between my boss and I.

The next day at work, I practiced courage. "Hey, I was curious if we could follow up about our conversation in the office yesterday. Is there a time that you'd be available to talk?" I could see the surprise on her face. She wasn't used to me initiating her like this. "Absolutely," she responded. At the end of the day, we sat in the empty office and I shared honestly about how I'd felt exposed talking about sensitive issues in front of everyone. Understanding unfolded itself between us. "Hannah, I am so sorry. I never meant to embarrass you. I should have asked to speak to you privately. Please forgive me." Trust was being rebuilt.

My manager went on to ask if she could speak into the places she was trying to address the day before. She corrected my assumption and shared where she saw that I was stuck in a pattern of not being able to receive good things. She pointed out behavior she'd seen that was connected to a belief that I was always in lack. Ultimately, I did need to hear what she had to say, but I needed to hear it in a way that felt safe. It was the redo we both needed, and it wouldn't have happened if I hadn't gone against the grain of my tendencies and owned how I felt.

I want to challenge you to take an honest inventory of your heart. Do you tend to stuff what you're feeling and avoid confrontation? Do you have a tendency to assume you're always in the wrong and avoid speaking up for yourself? Can you identify when you've been wronged? Jesus doesn't ask for us to become passive people. He wants us to be powerful people—kind *and* honest, loving *and* vulnerable.

WHEN YOU WEAR PERFORMANCE

Keys to Overcoming Performance
BY ABIGAIL ROLLINS

A beautiful stack of thirty hand-cut journals from an expensive hide sits on the table. I collect them and walk them over to my manager, Rosemary. *She's going to be so proud of me; I cut them perfectly. I'm going to be the best intern this leather department has ever seen.* I hand the stack over to her, beaming. She looks down at the journals, then back up at me full of compassion. "Abby, these were cut with the wrong template."

My mind starts buzzing. *Oh no! What a stupid mistake. This job was so simple. How did I get it wrong? What if they ask me to leave?* Everything that seems important suddenly comes crashing down around me: my pride, my ability to prove that I am the best—or at least my ability to prove that I am better than the other intern working with me. Rosemary forgives me, but I struggle to forgive myself, replaying the mistake over and over in my mind. Failing means that I am a failure.

This moment was the wake up call I needed.

All I've wanted to do my whole life is impress people. Performance was the outfit I wore when I built my highly qualified resumé and when I walked into my first corporate job interview. Day after day, year after year, I dressed myself in performance until I subconsciously believed that I am what I do. This was the same outfit I wore for the first month of my leather internship. But on this particular day, the day I mistakenly cut thirty unusable journals, Rosemary challenged me to consider whether this belief was still serving me. Was performance really what I wanted to wear every day?

Changing patterns requires making a plan. I began to dream by asking myself, *What would it look like for me to be powerful in these moments?* Then Rosemary and I created an action plan that looked like this: pause, take a deep breath, reflect, express your need and continue in joy. This plan has empowered me to believe that I am more than what I do. I have practiced this action plan repeatedly over the past couple of years and I am a better employee, leader and friend because of it. Not because of my performance, but because I am quick to love myself and receive the love of the Father.

Whenever I found myself struggling with obsessive thoughts like, *I have to do this perfect or else*, I would pause and practice. So many times, Rosemary would look me in the eyes after she saw me following through and say, "You've got this, Abby." It was in those moments I encountered the playful confidence of the Lord in Rosemary's actions. She didn't interrupt me to save the day, she was proud of me for following through with the plan and telling me in her encouragement and eye contact, *I'm proud of you, you are growing, you are believing you are worth the work.* I could feel her silent prayers filling me with energy to fight for myself. I am so thankful that I had a leader who gave me space to grow and practice and change before her eyes.

Closing thoughts by
JUSTINA STEVENS

You can't give grace to others without first giving grace to yourself. All of the staff that our interns encountered throughout this series have been practicing honest communication with the Lord about their failures and mistakes for years. Through asking the Lord questions and opening up to Him, they have learned how to receive the Lord's forgiveness and kind communication. And from that place, they have been able to extend forgiveness and kindness to others. It is unrealistic to think that you can become a clear and compassionate communicator without first receiving the Lord's compassion and insight. One key that our dear friend Graham Cooke has taught us is the power of asking good questions, especially in seasons of tension, frustration or failure. Initiating these kinds of conversations with the Lord is the first step in becoming an assertive communicator.

QUESTIONS

God, what can you be for me in this season that you couldn't be for me in any other time?

What does this situation mean for our relationship? What must I do to partner with you?

If Jesus were actually living in me, how would He handle this situation?

If Jesus were looking out through my eyes, how would He see this situation? This person? This battle?

What part of yourself are you opening up to me?

How are you turning this problem into a possibility?

What are you growing in me at this time?

How does this situation upgrade my position in the Spirit? Who am I becoming in Christ?

How is the favor of God working to my benefit through this situation?

If I believe what God is saying to me now, what are the outcomes for me at this point in my life?

If God believes this about me, what are the implications for Him in walking it out with me?

PROMPT

Take out your journal and write down a problem you are facing. Then, take a deep breath and invite the Holy Spirit to come help. Choose one of the questions above to invite God's perspective into your current situation. You never know what the Father has in mind for your growth, for your heart and story. He is ready to make beauty burst from ashes.

SHARING SPACES

BY SYDNEE MELA / PHOTOGRAPH BY MORGAN CAMPBELL

LIVING WITH PEOPLE IS HARD. NO ONE AFFECTS US AS MUCH AS THOSE WE LIVE WITH, THE ONES WHO SHARE OUR MOST FAMILIAR AND PERSONAL SPACES. THERE ARE WAYS TO HIDE, BUT A PERSON'S PRESENCE IN A HOUSE IS ALWAYS FELT. WE ARE MESSY, CLEAN, LOUD, QUIET, ACTIVE, LAZY, PASSIVE, AGGRESSIVE AND ALL THESE ELEMENTS COLLIDE WITH THOSE AROUND US. FOR ME, STAYING CONNECTED THROUGH THE TENSION OF LIVING WITH ROOMMATES HAS FORCED ME TO LEARN TO USE MY VOICE.

In my twenties, I moved out of my family home and started living with friends. I thought it would be the dream life. A house full of belly laughs, game nights and dinner parties. Everything would just fall into place. But living with people doesn't "just fall into place." We all have a different idea of home and comfort. We have different rhythms of eating, resting, entertaining, and in this case, cleaning. For the first time, I found myself unexpectedly excited to vacuum and tidy. Cleaning gave me a satisfying sense of ownership in my new house. But months passed by and life got busy for everyone. Dishes started piling in the sink, the living room got crowded with random belongings and the grime on the bathroom surfaces had the slight resemblance of sandpaper. Eventually, I became so uncomfortable and distracted by the dirty house that I couldn't relax. So I cleaned. At first, I didn't mind. But then week after week, a cycle developed. The house continued to get dirty and I continued to clean. *This isn't my mess to clean, I don't want to clean it up again, but it can't stay like this.* As I kept taking on this responsibility, my internal dialogue was getting more and more resentful. I started withdrawing to my room and avoiding my roommates. I had a growing desire to be anywhere else but home.

Does this scenario sound familiar to you? Have you ever found yourself caught in a cycle of making a mess you rarely clean, or cleaning up a mess you rarely make? In my twenties, I thought the problem was my roommates, that they were dismissing the mess and refusing to clean. But really, the biggest problem was my silence. I was comfortable avoiding; to me it was safer and easier. I avoided confrontation for a long time by managing the world around me and hiding my anger and pain. Ultimately, I was afraid to communicate and I chose to remain passive. Passivity is behavior led by the belief that "You matter, I don't." If conflict came up in my life, I would get quiet and comply. When I was hurt, I wouldn't talk about it.

Many of us believe that speaking up and confronting a problem creates more tension and more work. But in reality, it's often passivity that causes greater tension, distance and pain. My own resistance to addressing a problem only creates a bigger problem. Each time I withhold my honesty from my roommates, I cause them more pain by shutting them out and not allowing them to love me. I end up punishing them with silence for not meeting my unspoken expectations. But no one can meet an unspoken need.

Passivity created distance in the relationships that mattered the most to me. *This isn't working. I have to do something.* I started with writing a simple text: "Hey guys, can we meet up? I'd like to talk about our house. Would there be a good time to connect?" We met. I opened up and shared. In contrast to my fears, I was met with understanding. My roommates received me. We made a plan to care for the house. I was surprised by the perspective everyone brought. What amazed me most was how a simple conversation affected my own heart. Hearing my roommates' thoughts gave me understanding, even compassion. It was freeing to finally express what I'd kept hidden. And my bravery opened the door for me to be seen and known.

We all have this choice—to open our hearts, use our voices and draw close. This is something I continue to practice. I don't do it perfectly. I constantly ask the Holy Spirit for help. Now that I'm in my thirties, living with roommates looks drastically different. I see the reward of talking through tense moments and finding deeper connection on the other side. I live with greater bravery and truer peace. But that has taken a lot of time and effort. Not all my conversations end with joy and celebration; some still end unresolved, with frustration and tears. But success isn't found in the outcome. Success is found in what is steadily growing in my friendships: Bravery. Honesty. Connection.

PROMPT: Are there places where you have given into passivity with a roommate or close friend? Get out your journal and complete a Communication Tool (see pg. 78) about the last time you felt frustrated, shut down or you lost your peace around this person and you responded with passivity. Don't be afraid to talk about this with the Holy Spirit; He wants to help you. Once you complete your Communication Tool, ask Him, "Holy Spirit, what is my next step?" Perhaps it's simply to pray for them, or to own where you've been unkind or inconsistent. Perhaps it is to initiate a conversation about what you need or where you've been hurt. Receive the Holy Spirit's courage to follow through with this step.

ASKING FOR he

by MORGAN CAMPBELL

I ALWAYS BELIEVED that striving and pushing my way to the top would lead to the success and growth I was seeking in my life. If I worked hard and looked like I had everything together, I could make it. But it turned out that pushing through life, ignoring my problems and needs with the hope that they'd eventually go away, only left me burned out and exhausted. I desired sustainability and growth, but I didn't know how to find it. If I wanted to change, I realized I had to reach out and ask for help, something that just so happened to be one of my greatest fears. I was naturally more self-sufficient, and had plenty of reasons not to reach out: *I'm going to be too much. No one else struggles with this but me. I should have already dealt with this a long time ago.* It's a vulnerable thing to open up our weaknesses to someone else; it confronts our independence and control. And there's the risk of rejection, *What if they say no?* Most of us think that if we're in need of help, we're in a bad place. But the truth is if we're asking for guidance, it's a sign that we're healthy. It's human to need help; it's something we never outgrow. While receiving someone's feedback wasn't always comfortable, it was exactly what I needed. One of the best decisions I made was to lay down my pride and reach out for help. Here are some keys I've learned for inviting others to speak into my life:

Take Initiative.

Asking for help requires taking initiative. We can't expect people to read our minds or offer unsolicited advice. Take time to think of a few people in your life whom you trust, look up to and who challenge you. Consider what part of your life you need help with, and who has wisdom and authority in that area. While we all want to have time with people we admire the most—a lead pastor, a worship leader, someone you may watch on a global stage—don't underestimate the "regular" people in your life; they have more to offer than you may think. The first person you ask might not have the answer, but don't give up. Everyone will bring their own experience to the table. Whether these people turn into leaders in your life or it's a one-time moment, twenty minutes with someone can affect you profoundly if you're humble and willing to receive.

Ask for & Receive Feedback.

Being led requires that you ask for and receive the hard truth. Asking questions like, "How has my behavior affected you?" or, "Do you see any places in my life where I can grow?" are amazing ways to start the conversation. Whenever you're given feedback, you can expect to face your pride. You always have a choice to either get defensive with excuses and justifications ("Why are you bringing this up? It's not my fault because…") or to respond with a soft heart ("I'm going to really pray about that, thank you for being honest"). Give yourself grace to not know answers. Take the advice you've been given and sit with the Lord. Not everyone's advice will be helpful. Always spend time with the Lord and submit the advice you've been given to Him.

Reject Entitlement.

Remember that the people you are reaching out to live full lives. They are moms, dads, wives, husbands, friends and co-workers. When I started reaching out for help, I had to recognize that I was not the center of their lives, and I wasn't supposed to be. There have been times when the person I've reached out to has twenty minutes after their kids have gone to sleep, or ten minutes on the phone while they're on their way to work, and it was just what I needed. If you begin to feel entitled to others' time, I encourage you to start practicing gratitude. This slight shift in thinking will change every interaction into a gift. It's important to lay down your ideals about what a moment of vulnerability and advice is supposed to look like. Being flexible, even when it isn't the "perfect" atmosphere, opens up the door to receive help in the midst of daily life.

Be a Blessing.

When others take time to intentionally love me, it is important for me to show love back. I encourage you to ask the Holy Spirit for ways you can specifically pour back into your leaders. Reflect on where they might feel empty or tired in this season, and think creatively about how you can sow back in. I remember feeling so much gratitude for one of my leaders and having a deep desire to give back to her. I wrote her a card, read it out loud to her and offered to babysit her kids. She was a new mom and I knew that this act of service would communicate love and fill her up. Find out ways that you can communicate your love to strengthen your connection and express gratitude. Maybe it's buying them flowers, getting them a gift card to their favorite restaurant, helping with yard work or washing their car. Think outside the box!

Prepare.

Be a powerful communicator. If you've reached out for help and the person has agreed to make time for you, it's your responsibility to know what you want to talk about. Write down two or three clear questions that you would like to ask. I strongly encourage you to be as specific as possible—don't beat around the bush! If you have a question, just ask it and don't waste time.

Prompt.

I've been consistently asking for help for the last five years. Inviting others to speak into my life can still be uncomfortable for me but the reward of my brave choice is that I am becoming the truest version of myself. I have a limited view of who I can become, but when I ask for help, greater possibilities of change are within reach. People are able to give you what you can't give yourself. Be brave as you seek out help.

Ask the Lord to highlight people in your life who carry qualities that you admire. Make a list of potential people that could speak into your life. Pray and ask the Lord who you should initiate contact with and then reach out. It will take courage, vulnerability and maybe a few different tries but your heart is worth the risk!

SPEAKING INTO PEOPLE'S

by JUSTINA STEVENS

I'VE BEEN RUNNING with Melissa and Jonathan since I was a teenager. Melissa's relationship with the Holy Spirit and the way I could hear the Father's tone in Jonathan's voice left such an impression on me at seventeen. They both had a way with words, always looking me in the eyes in a way that returned dignity back to my young heart. Through their love and leadership, I've learned to love and lead, and for the past decade, I've had the honor of pioneering schools, pastoring and establishing art departments alongside them. One of my greatest privileges is leading others. I love sitting with students and staff and helping them navigate through their lives, giving them feedback and leading them for extended seasons of time. This part of my job has brought me to the height of joy and awe of what God can do with a willing heart. It has also taken me to the edge of myself, where I've felt more frustrated and clueless than I can explain.

Loving people is no small thing. It costs you mental and emotional capacity and requires dependency on the Holy Spirit. Truly loving cannot happen without a willingness to empathize with all kinds of pain, grief, joy and triumph. For many of you readers, you may not be in a job like mine. Some of you are full-time mothers, doctors, architects or accountants. We all have different capacities to bring to the table, but I think we all have a common desire: to affect people, and to love with the kind of love Jesus modeled. My desire is to impart some wisdom for speaking into people's lives. Whether it be a one-time occurrence or for an extended season, these keys are incredibly helpful in navigating through the beautiful waters of helping people.

Follow Joy.

The Lord may be pinpointing a person you have the authority to speak into: someone you are ahead of in life and in maturity. Perhaps it's a young adult or a couple that just got married. When you see them, you may feel a desire to connect or reach out—these feelings can be an amazing indicator that you have something to give from your own experience and relationship with Jesus. I would encourage you to initiate them, ask them over for dinner or ask if there is a way you can support them.

If someone asks you for advice or help and you feel uneasy about it, don't give a default answer. Ask yourself, *Why?* Is it because you've never helped someone before and it's uncharted territory? Or is it because you don't have capacity or joy to make time for this person? If it's the first, survey your heart. Did you ask the Lord to help you make an impact? Did you ask the Lord for purpose? Perhaps He's answering it through this person's initiation. If it's the second, kindly communicate that in this season it's not a possibility and bless them to keep reaching out to others.

Ask Questions and Don't Be Afraid to Kindly Interrupt.

When speaking into someone's life, don't hesitate to ask questions so that they can come to conclusions. The solution can seem obvious or simple to you when giving advice, but it's probably not so for the person you're meeting with. Questions are an amazing way to help a person identify how they feel and help you connect with them. You may also find that the person you're connecting with is talking so much that it's difficult to follow. Don't be afraid to kindly interject with a question, "If I could stop you there for a minute, it sounds like you're processing a lot right now. I'm curious if you could think of one thing you'd like to focus on today?" Or, "Could I interject here? From what I've heard you say, it seems like you don't really need anything. Can you pinpoint a question that I can help you with?" These questions may seem abrupt, but they are amazing ways to create boundaries around your time and capacity and when delivered in a kind tone, they are very helpful to the person you are meeting with.

You Cannot Work Harder Than Them.

If someone seeks you out for help, it's really important to recognize that the only ones who can initiate true change in their life are them and the Lord. You are not the savior of anyone's story. For example, if you are sitting down with someone that really struggles with depression, comparison, fear or anxiety, you do not have what it takes to make it okay. You can help them identify unhealthy patterns and find solutions, you can pray for them and you can encourage them. But at the end of the day, they have to want freedom. I cannot tell you how many young adults I've tried to drag into transformation without even realizing it. Growth takes a lot of work and if someone doesn't want to do it, they don't have to. When giving someone advice, remember, it's their responsibility to listen and apply it.

You Don't Have To Know All The Answers.

If you're in a moment when someone's asked you a question that you don't know how to answer, that's okay! Admitting you don't know and then inviting them to pray with you for direction from the Holy Spirit is powerful. He is the Spirit of Truth, who you both depend on! Pray a simple prayer out loud and then pay attention. Does a picture come to either of your minds? Do either of you hear a word? Perhaps neither of you hear anything. In that case, prompt them to spend some time with the Lord that week and ask Him again. Remember, God wants all of us to be free more than we do; He will speak.

You Are Valuable and Your Feelings Matter.

If a person schedules time and cancels repeatedly, or tends to interrupt you when you're giving advice, or makes pointed remarks that hurt you, it is important to communicate how their behavior is affecting you. You are not bulletproof, and your feelings matter right alongside theirs. It isn't wrong to kindly communicate how their behavior is affecting you. A great way to communicate your feelings is saying, "Could I give you some feedback?" After they've agreed, open up. You do not need to diminish yourself or them to get a point across. "I noticed that you've canceled our get-togethers via text three times. That was tough for me. I need to feel valuable, and sudden cancelations without a clear explanation communicate that you don't care about my time or my plans. Is that what you are trying to communicate?" And let them respond. Or you could try, "When I hear you say, 'I know,' after I give you advice, I'm puzzled why you've asked for help. If you knew, why are you reaching out to me for help?" Moments like these are some of the most powerful because you get to share your experience and it gives them space to respond. When I've given people feedback in kindness, it has built trust, opened up communication and illuminated places that the person didn't even know they needed help.

    I pray that these keys would fill you with inspiration to be a powerful person and affect those around you. Remember, no one has all the answers except Jesus! Let this truth liberate you to take risks and love well.

Twelve years ago, my wife Holly and I moved our family to Kona, Hawaii and joined the mission of Loren and Darlene Cunningham, the founders of YWAM. We are part of the Executive Team that leads our Kona campus. Kona's campus is huge and functions like a small university; we have about 600 full-time staff and 700 students coming into the campus every quarter for discipleship training. We've found that it's essential to have clear values for what we're doing. For us, Jesus' model is the greatest standard. Jesus showed the world the only way of leadership: servant leadership. I think as Christians there are places where we've gotten a bit off, believing there is a difference between leadership and servant leadership. Really, there is only one kind that Jesus modeled. Day in and day out with His disciples and those who were considered unlovable He laid down His life. He was a servant leader, who never operated in a different realm of leadership. Loren and Darlene, Holly and I and our entire Leadership Team model this type of leadership from the top down. We all are a part of this volunteer mission, we all raise financial support and we all are choosing connection with God and each other. These simple, powerful choices alone naturally affect anyone that comes near us and has caused a beautiful thing to begin to happen: we're creating a culture. Culture is like weather—you can't be unaffected by it. If enough people are in agreement over the culture it is powerful. If you have a couple hundred people who are reflecting eternal summer and a new person is reflecting rain, that rainy attitude just won't last very long. That one person can't overcome the several hundred reflections of summer. In the same vein, no individual is stronger than the collective culture of servanthood and the teachings of Jesus we've embraced. I would love to share with you a few of our other values for culture at YWAM, Kona.

1. Connection to the Great Commission

At YWAM, we have a core value that all of our communities are centered around the presence of God. We are inspired by the church of Acts and their strength in worship, prayer, teaching, intercession, breaking bread and communion. When we read Acts we see patterns of the early church waiting on God and ministering to the Lord. In the same way, we encourage all of our communities to have a strong emphasis on worship, prayer and the centrality of the presence of God.

For us, directly connected to that is a value that our communities be focused on the Great Commission. This is what keeps us from turning inward and becoming self-centered. For our mission, it is absolutely essential that we be focused on extending the Kingdom of God. We've built this mission around the Great Commission passage in Matthew 28, but also around the call to "preach the Gospel to every creature" (Mark 16:15, NKJV), and around Isaiah 60:1 and 3 (NIV): "Arise, shine, for your light has come, and the glory of the Lord rises upon you…Nations will come to your light, and kings to the brightness of your dawn." These passages have informed our priority for extending the Kingdom and staying connected to the Great Commission.

We believe that communities are healthiest when they are centered on His presence, and when their mission, purpose and cause is fulfilling the Great Commission. We see this throughout history—from the Clapham sect, to the Moravians, to the Methodist awakening, to the Circuit Rider movement. All of these communities carried a value for the presence of God and the Great Commission.

by ANDY BYRD

2. Freedom to fail with an appropriate response

We have six children, and when my kids first learned to walk I celebrated their first steps like it was the greatest victory in all of history. I was so excited they were learning to take some steps even though they fell down often. I'd be a terrible dad if I punished my child for failing to walk properly after one step. In the same way, I'd be a terrible dad if I never empowered and encouraged them to take more steps. Our desire as leaders is to keep a balance between challenging and encouraging, because people need both to succeed. The only way to see growth in our communities and in discipleship is to celebrate victories, as small as they may be, while also having grace for failure and a plan for an appropriate response. We've chosen not to be afraid of the truth, but to press into it. The beauty and difficulty of community lies in blending together a freedom to fail and a high value for an appropriate response.

I think that most ministries tend to have a lean, either toward grace or to response. This is normal. Grace-driven ministries are excellent at forgiveness, compassion and connection. When someone fails, they are quick to love, forgive and move on. Response-driven ministries are excellent at empowerment. They acknowledge the reality of a situation and aren't afraid of the sobering emotions that come with it. Both of these elements are essential to a thriving community. Grace alone will not lead to breakthrough or change. Response alone will leave people feeling disconnected and unloved. However, grace matched with appropriate responses is powerful. Repentance is the appropriate response to sin. That doesn't mean weeping, gnashing teeth or ripping our clothes. It really can be joyful, because repentance is the removal of obstacles to intimacy. When our YWAM team blends these two things, we see our staff and students walking in such maturity, all because they were loved and championed by truth into their breakthrough.

3. People following their dreams

We have an ethos to champion greatness and God-given destinies in the people we are leading. If there is a dream in their heart and their character matches the responsibility it will require to walk that dream out, we encourage them to go for it. Loren was among the first missionaries to go to Korea and impart a vision for sending out Korean missionaries, not just receiving them. Now Korea is the second largest mission-sending nation in the world. Before Loren had been there, they hadn't sent out any missionaries. We have a heart to empower people to answer God's call on their lives whether that's within YWAM or in a different capacity.

I don't think any of us would want to be a part of a community that just looked inward. A community that tinkers with itself constantly and just tries to make a little bit better version of itself is boring. There's got to be something better to live for than just getting along and being good. Healthy communities look at the needs around them and ask, "Out of the strength of our love, commitment and Biblical lifestyles, how do we impact others around us to bring them into the same love and Kingdom reality we share and are living in?"

PROMPT: Whether you're a part of a large or small community, gather with your closest group of friends to have a conversation. Which one of these three areas above do you feel inspired to grow in? Open up and talk with your friends for how you can grow in connection in this specific area. We encourage you to take an honest inventory of the culture of your friendship or Small Group. Allow the Holy Spirit to cast vision for new values.

GENEROSITY

"WHOEVER BRINGS BLESSING WILL BE ENRICHED, AND ONE WHO WATERS WILL HIMSELF BE WATERED."
PROVERBS 11:25

SECTION 03

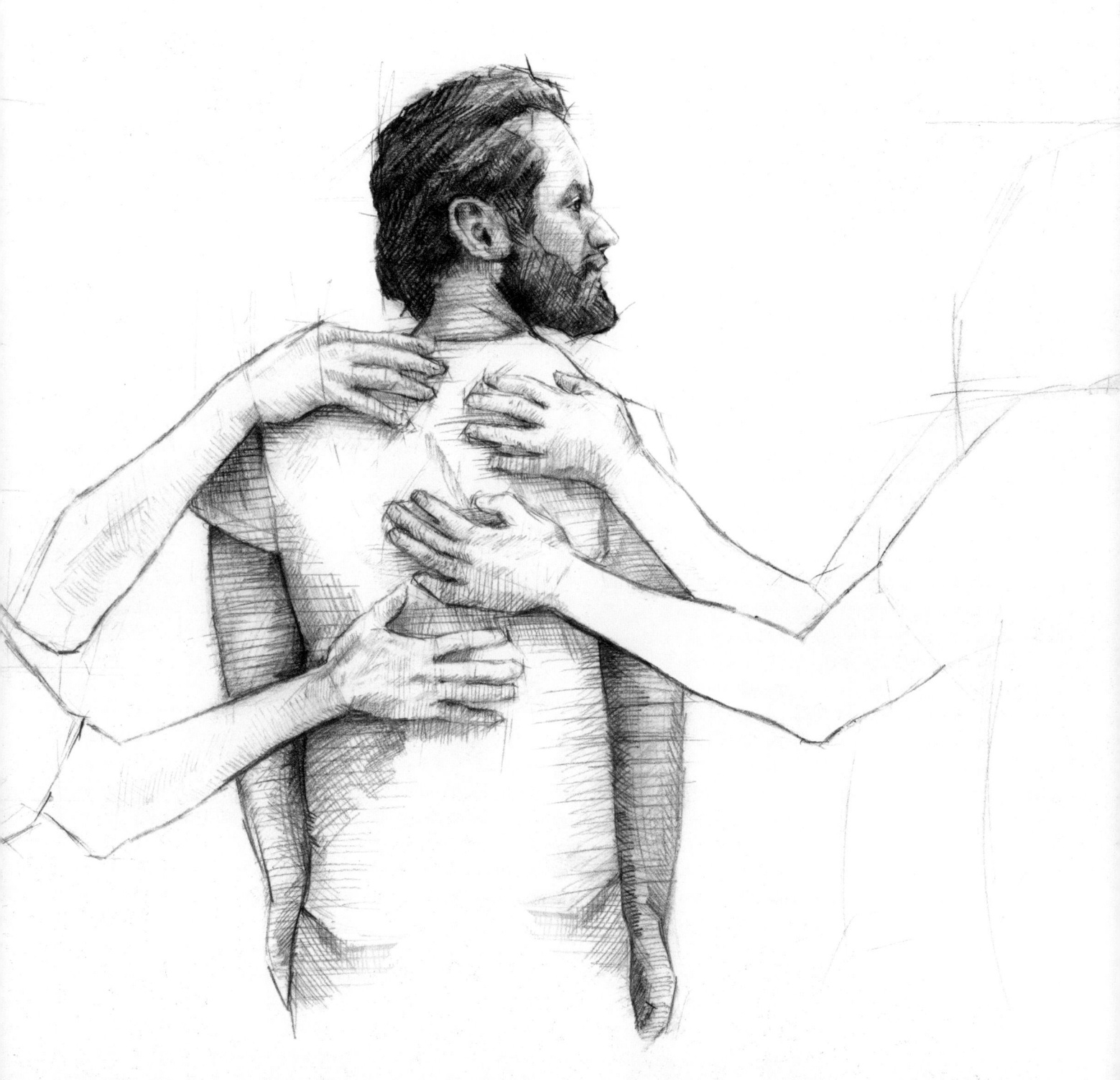

by PHYLLIS UNKEFER
photography by LUCAS SANKEY

range of COLOR

I have always lived in places that were peopled with a range of color. White father. Black mother. A black mother with a deep complexion. A white father with German roots and a red-tinged beard. A black mother with cowry shells in her dreadlocks. A white father with The Police or Tom Petty in the car tape deck.

My parents invited both their families to summer picnics at Patriarch Park. For me, those picnics have all coalesced into one memory. Between the smell of charcoal, hanging upside down on the swings and every known cousin piling onto a merry-go-round with our laughter spilling over the sides—between all that, my memory centers on one sight: Two yellow lawn chairs in the shade, slightly angled together, where my grandfather and Great Aunt Ida sit. His white hands resting on his knees. Her black hands gesturing gently, like shadows of the inflections in her voice. They sit and laugh and talk awhile. Maybe it's the gravity of retrospection that gives this image depth, but somehow, even as a nine-year-old girl, I noticed and never forgot.

I grew up around a range of color. Brown siblings. A spectrum of neighbors. Diverse schools. Not excluding my high school, where the black kids hung out in the foyer, the white kids in the commons, the Latinos by the double doors and the Asians by the lockers up the hall. We did in the early 2000s have ways of crossing these social red tapes. If we sat side by side in geometry class or found ourselves on the same floor hockey team in gym, we'd slip into a friendly banter, making jokes to defend ourselves from the common enemy of our boredom and realizing soon enough that we all liked the same rap songs. Plenty of us didn't oppose friendship with different shades. But so many of us still somehow gravitated back to our comfortable habitats: black kids in the foyer, white kids in the commons, Latinos by the double doors, Asians up the hall.

Comfortability is a human pursuit. So understood the inventors of air conditioning, lullabies and those cushy reclining movie theater seats. One source of human comfort is culture. The Father knew at the time of the Tower of Babel that when He sent people their separate ways with a jigsaw puzzle of new words on their tongues, a diversity of cultures and races would emerge. That when we spread out across the world, colder climates would blond our hair and, for the sake of surviving winter, teach us to revere time with careful punctuality. That warmer climates would maintain our melanin and, with no threat of winter, give us less reason to rush through life and therefore start all our parties two hours late. (Please excuse my sweeping generalizations.) I don't think this was a coincidence. I think God was inspired by beauty when He scattered people from Babel, and His deep longing for diversity. He wanted an array of color to reflect the different sides of His face. And for every pocket of humanity, He designed the gift of culture. Culture is a meeting place for human beings. A table where connection is nurtured by what we share: common language, foods, birthday songs and inside jokes. Our slang, our jumprope chants, our Christmas carols that return every year like migrating birds, our Eucharist bread and wine, which beat we clap on, the candles we light or the brooms we jump over at weddings. Culture, for better or worse, helps us understand what's expected of us. Culture offers us rhythms of belonging. And that is a source of comfort.

I have a deep need for belonging. So do you. Every time I've moved cities or walked into a new community, I've felt the nervous and vulnerable question of my belonging. *Who are these people, and how do I relate to them? Which direction will friendship come from? What social virtue will be celebrated here, and will I know how to do that dance?* Unspoken questions like these gathered inside me when I moved to North Carolina. Here at a small school in the middle of the woods, I found a little less color than I was accustomed to. I was coming into a mostly white community. Among the staff, I was the only person with darker skin. When their social media featured a lot of flannel, leather boots and thick mountain-man-ish facial hair, I could have digested a handful of preconceived theories about who they'd be and whether I'd fit in. But so much of that was swept away when I arrived and stayed awhile; eclipsed by their kindness and their eye contact and their genuine words.

So, I stayed a while longer. For years, I'd asked Jesus to teach me what binds up the brokenhearted, and here I'd entered a culture that was pursuing wholeness of the heart. I wanted to stay. I was invited to join staff and I felt the joy to. But even with all my good reasons, I'd be dishonest if I said I never felt a tug—the same tug that drew all my fellow high schoolers to their respective corners. The tug to surround myself with people who look like me. The tug that tightened my chest at night and pressed the question of whether or not I wanted to be shaped by a mostly white community. It surprised me. I grew up with a white father, white grandparents, white aunts and uncles who kept their love for me in plain sight. All the afternoons I sat in a kitchen chair as my Scotch-Irish grandmother hummed and toasted me an English muffin with melted cheese gave me little reason to question my comfortability in a white community. But I still felt it. So, I had to follow it to its root; had to peel open my hesitation to name the real fear.

The Holy Spirit is the One who sees the deepest. When I asked Him for clarity, He tapped His finger on the matter of pain. Among the things shared by culture—dance moves, hairstyles, when or when not to laugh—there is also a common reservoir of pain. Collective pain. Pain that seeps up through history and threads itself into the present. I had pain that was passed down to me. From my black grandparents' lives in the segregated South. From my great grandmother whose son was killed for dating a woman with lighter skin. From my mother when her high school put on the musical, *Oklahoma*, and gave the lead role to someone vocally weak but the preferred shade. Every culture has pain. I'm not saying that we stay victimized by that pain; the Cross is too radical and Jesus has too great a means for us to heal. But we may not notice our unprocessed pain until it spills into sight. For me, it came up as fear. When I joined this community, I was afraid that I might have to hide parts of myself. Might need to dance around the subject of race to prevent making someone uncomfortable. I was afraid that in some overt or subtle way, I might experience proof of a notion that one of my races might still not truly care about the other. To some, that fear may sound irrational, to others it's familiar. And that difference itself is another source of the tug—we find comfort in shared viewpoints, shared awarenesses, shared fears. There's a kind of intimacy there, where we're inclined to stay among our own people, because it's where we feel the most known. Jesus was fully aware of my fears when He brought me to this community. And He gently asked me to stay.

So, I stayed. Not just physically, or with my reluctance, but I stayed with my mind, my ears, my words. I stayed and chose the people in front of me. There were the usual ways of building trust: through good questions, late night ice cream, the slow familiarity of sitting side by side on a couch. Wading through conflict without getting shipwrecked. Shy secrets offered and reverently kept. And the kind of Friday night laughter that one's legs cannot bear up under and reduces us to a pile of joyful hysteria on the floor. There were other ways of building trust; I opened my culture to them like the lid of a jewelry box. My white friends delved into 90s hiphop with me, and allowed me to explain the high treason of "ashiness" on black skin (hence the bottle of lotion inside every black woman's purse, glove box and half the drawers in her house). Those who were my closest friends approached racially-charged events in the news with me. Their questions about my experience as a woman of color were unhurried and intended to understand. In this country, members of a minority tend to carry the belief, whether or not consciously, that the greater majority does not truly care about them, a belief that

> **And before I realized it, Jesus was mending something in me. Because when there's a range of color, there's a range of healing.**

out of broken parts of our country's story, implications in the media and experiences both real and amplified by broken trust. So, when a white friend asks about my racial experience with non-assumption and genuine tenderness, Jesus mends something inside of me. He reverses my fears. This is not a case of white heroism, nor are these instances any more powerful than my moments of connection with someone black—neither white nor black people are the saviors of my story. It's Jesus, the One who expanded my nine-year-old mind just enough to see the holiness in my grandfather and great aunt sitting together under a tree.

Most people I've met have never asked Jesus about the matter of their race. I'm not talking about theological philosophizing about the social construct. I mean getting quiet enough to let Him speak to our own deep, past-the-head-to-the-heart beliefs about our racial identities. I remember the first time I let His voice pour into this part of me. It was years ago, when I'd been hitting some snags in my identity. I admitted to Him that I felt the pressure of expectation—that mixed-girl fear of not fully meeting either cultural expectation, black or white (now, whether or not those expectations were as real or as narrow as they felt is a whole other conversation). I asked Him what His expectations were instead, and the volume of His thoughts surprised me. You know when you've asked Him the question He's been waiting to answer and He has an amazing amount to say?

His words came flooding in, brimming over in my thoughts. He stated that those expectations weren't His. That He enjoyed my spiraling hair. That inside me, He'd made a meeting place of two entirely different family lines. And that He'd always intended a double portion—rather than not belonging in either, I could delight in belonging in both. Jesus' voice mends me. What He's mending most, like stitches closing up a wound, is my sense of belonging.

I have a deep need for belonging. And it's required me to stay. To stay in one place demands sacrifice; the laying down of every other option to be present for just one. But I'm finding that God never allows sacrifice to go unmet. He always chases it with some kind of redemption, some kind of unexpected blooming. It started with one. Then two. Then five more. Young black women, just a few at a time, found their way to our school. They later said they'd all done a dance on the inside when they first saw each other, thrilled at the error in their assumption that they'd be the only black person here. That same rush of delight followed me as I watched their journeys unfold. It's not that we set out to address the matter of race, it's just that God does what He wants to do. And He evidently wants His Kingdom to come into every part of us, not excluding our cultures or races. So, I sat across tables from them. When their questions of identity surfaced, I told them to let the Father's voice define them and sink into the hidden cracks of who they are. They listened for Him. He always spoke, full of warmth, affirming their true selves, their significance, the shades of their skin. Years ago, I'd wept with Jesus over the contemptuous relationship between black women and their hair, and now I was looking into a black girl's eyes, inviting her to ask Him what He thinks of her un-straightened, unprocessed, natural hair. His adoring words washed her head like oil. More striking still is that back when I first came to this school, I was too afraid to focus an assignment on the Harriet Tubman painting at an art museum, for fear of being "typical". But these women were standing up, openly offering their stories to the whole community. One admitted, "I knew what it was as a nine-year-old to grind up chalk and rub it on my skin hoping to take the melanin away..." But then they testified of how fully the Holy Spirit can heal, and they sang their self-acceptance: *I too am made in the image of God.*

Their process brought me to tears as much as it did them. And at the same time, a specific beauty emerged in my community. When our students of color opened their cultures, without excluding the pain, I was moved by everyone's response. They honored it. Made room for it. Welcomed, affirmed and cried over it. They rejoiced at the depth of what God was doing. This community celebrated them *in* their racial identity, not in spite of it. True belonging will only exist where there's acknowledgment of who we fully are. I watched my community acknowledge them, and before I realized it, Jesus was mending something in me. Because when there's a range of color, there's a range of healing. I then understood one part of why He asked me to stay. It's a step beyond comfort to be together with those who are different. But what I knew even at nine years old is that togetherness is holy. Togetherness, permeated with love, heals. It's a range of color that looks the most like God.

every little thing

by JESSIE MILLER
photograph by MORGAN CAMPBELL

Are you tired of loving others?

Do you ever want to give up, pull back and save the "good stuff" for those you know will appreciate it? Have you ever been pushed to the end of your own love's capacity? When I started my career as a high school biology teacher, I came to realize very quickly that my good intentions wouldn't be enough. If I wanted to love *every* teenager who came through my door, even the ones who pushed me away, I would have to connect to the Source of Love deeper than I ever had before. What I brought to the table as a person, a teacher and a lover of God was powerful but in my desire to love well, I was also vulnerable. The students mattered to me. Bad attitudes, selfish behavior, disappointing test scores and hurtful interactions affected me. *I'm trying so hard God. Does it even matter?*

The Lord never asks us to love without His help—instead, He asks us to lean into *His* understanding, not our own. Self-pity and negativity are indicators that your love is seeking the wrong things. When I looked to my toughest students for constant affirmation that my love was working, I grew weary very quickly. Love doesn't always bear fruit before your eyes. Your actions can't be rooted in reward. God was offering me a different way of approaching connection, "What if you loved them because I love them? Would you be willing to serve the story I am writing in their life?" True love is humbling. "I know that hurt, but what do you think she believes about herself?" the Father would offer, after a student lashed out at me. "What if you said 'hi' even though they were rude yesterday?" He would whisper in the hall. "What if you didn't assume they were always bad?" He would challenge, as I saw certain names on my class roster. The Father adored every single student and was inviting me into *His* pursuit of their hearts. His love didn't only flow when they deserved it or were aware of it. The Trinity inspired me to notice the details of the human heart and never underestimate the power of little things.

"What if you always called them by name? You're going to be great with names. What if we brought them donuts for coming to class on time? They need something to look forward to. What if you crafted songs for them to sing? They love music so much." The Trinity's ideas for loving were endless. The quicker I said yes to "love them anyway" the faster the ideas came. "What if you wrote them each encouraging notes before their exam? What if you threw her a baby shower? What if you taught them about honor? What if you remembered his birthday?" Every little thing I tried mattered because I was trying it with Him. If you listen to the Trinity's ideas long enough, you'll start thinking everyone is lovable. His perspective rubs off on you. How can we not keep trying when we see how deep His affection for His children runs? No one is too far gone. God has a way to reach every single human soul. His love is brilliant and precise—and resolutely unconditional. We are the ones who hold back, not Him. We are the ones who give up when it feels like nothing is changing. We are the ones who think, *I've tried everything, Lord.*

What would happen if you left the results of your love in God's hands and just focused on what He was inspiring *you* to do? Only God knows the entirety of someone's story, and He is inviting you to let go of the need to understand your part before you play it. Weary love is rejuvenated when God's perspective is allowed to revive it. If you let Him, He will fill you with possibility when you feel empty and ready to give up. Trust me, you want to know the God who never runs out. To feel His love pulsing through your veins in the midst of adversity is to experience a miracle—a miracle available to all who will humble themselves and try. I love running into my old students and hearing what they remember about me or my class. I cherish the stories, the smiles of fondness, the gentle tears or a "man, I miss your class, it felt like home." I'll never know the exact effect I had on their lives. But, I do know that my love left them a little softer towards His love, and that was no small feat.

PROMPT: With whom have you grown weary? Where is God inviting you into a new, "What if…?" Maybe it's one person or maybe it's a larger group of people. Ask the Lord to fill you with *His* love. Ask Him to inspire you with new ideas. Create a list of "What ifs" and begin practicing them with the Father. Don't love with the goal of seeing tangible change in that person. Instead, take note of what happens in your heart when the Father's perspective about them becomes more real than your own. Every little thing can serve the stories God is writing in other people's lives.

BUILDING A TEAM THROUGH EXTRAVAGANCE

by CASS LANGTON
artwork by JUSTINA STEVENS

One of the most humbling moments

I can remember was during our 2014 Annual Hillsong Women's Conference, which was held in a big arena in Sydney, Australia. The stage was set, and rehearsals were in full swing. A mother grabbed me around the waist and held me close, tears streaming down her cheeks, a smile as wide as the ocean on her face. She kept repeating two words over and over to me: "Thank you. Thank you. Thank you." And when I asked what for, she simply said, "Thank you for seeing more in my son than he believed was in him. For loving him, for encouraging him and for championing him." You see, her son had spent years sleeping on a makeshift bed on an apartment floor; his brothers were in prison, and this mother feared for his future. Yet within her son was a heart for worship; he had the voice of an angel and the gift of a shepherd on his life. He had become a key part of our worship team at church and had started to dream for himself a future where God could use his life to impact the lives of others.

In the 1800s in California, and a long way away in the outback of Australia, a gold rush hit. People gave their lives away, risked everything and sacrificed greatly to go mining for gold. Some struck it rich, but many just searched far and wide for the illusive treasure, imagining a better reality for themselves. Sometimes I wonder if there is a gold rush waiting to happen again in the Church if only pastors and leaders had eyes to see the incredible wealth that the Lord has deposited within the Church for His glory. People are extraordinary. They are beautiful and talented, gifted and skilled, messy and complicated; and within them all is gold.

Ten years into my role as the Global Worship and Creative Pastor at Hillsong Church, I can honestly tell you it's been worth it—giving my life away, taking a risk and sacrificing it all in order to see the gold rise in the lives of others, their brilliance and uniqueness finding its fit within community. At Hillsong Church, I oversee a team of 25,000 volunteers. They come from different countries, different languages and different cultures; 10,500 of them live here in Australia. We meet weekly as a team to get ready for Sundays; each Thursday night we gather as a creative community to worship, hone in our creativity, learn and encourage each other and tell stories of what it looks like when God is at work amongst us. We dream and imagine. We seek God and endeavor to hear from Heaven in order to turn up on Sunday and lead a church in the pursuit of God. I've learned that it takes extravagant leadership to build a team of creatives. It takes extravagant encouragement to bring out the best in people, and it compounds in extravagant worship of our extravagant God.

There are a few key values that as a team we seek to exemplify. They are simple, obvious and probably need little explanation; however, I believe that they're fundamental in creating a team that is unified in purpose and in calling. The Bible is clear that where there is unity God commands a blessing.

YOU LOSE NOTHING BY CHAMPIONING OTHERS.

Sometimes it's easy to see everything as a pie: a finite measure, which once consumed, nothing is left over. But the Kingdom of God isn't a pie that runs out; it's a river that keeps flowing. There is always more; it changes and moves. I think opportunity and involvement for team and volunteers is best seen in that light. If we spend our whole lives protecting our piece of the pie we become jealous and possessive; but we are meant to live expansive lives, building each other up, offering encouragement, watching God at work and then calling the gold out in the people we lead. This creates more space at the table to which we have been so welcomed. Big leaders live invitational lives; they create room for people's gifts to flourish and space for expression. Big leaders are generous with the platforms that they have been given both literally and figuratively; they willingly share what they have been entrusted with. One of my greatest joys in life is to watch people find their wings and be allowed to contribute in their sweet spot (we call it their superpower). Recently I watched my beautiful friend, Jessie—who is a gifted writer and an incredibly beautiful human complete with social anxiety disorders—conquer her fear and tell her story in front of a room of 6,000 people. She spoke at our Annual Worship & Creative Conference in the most vulnerable, real way, and in doing so, released artists and creatives who also struggle with similar issues to feel heard. In sharing the platform and championing her, I didn't miss out, but gained incredibly as I watched many find peace.

BELIEVE IN PEOPLE MORE THAN THEY BELIEVE IN THEMSELVES.

We tend to see our own shortcomings more easily than we see our strengths. It's all a matter of perspective, and often we need people to come alongside of us with a highlighter pen to show us the good things in us—to call out qualities like loyalty and grace, kindness and joy, endurance and inner fortitude. It takes people to point out the gifts we naturally overlook in ourselves. No one comes ready-made; we are all works in progress, so finding a community where raw talent can be harnessed and nurtured is a gift. One of the most creative pursuits is having the foresight to see what may be. Unearthing someone's potential yields great reward. There's nothing like watching someone try and succeed for the first time, or the joy of standing back and watching someone discover—with a little more effort, a bit more practice, some coaching and encouragement—their perfect fit.

The first time Ben Hastings (a songwriter who contributed on the Hillsong Worship, Hillsong United and Hillsong Young & Free projects) brought an idea for a song to me, it had been the most incredible team night. We had talked about going "off grid," following the Holy Spirit into uncharted territory—about going into the dark, letting the Lord lead us where He willed. Marty Sampson had led worship that night with no words, no lyrics and no known songs—just instruments and free worship. At the end of that night, Ben tentatively approached me and posed a question. He asked, "Do you think we had no lyrics tonight because I was meant to give you a song that I've been sitting on?" He ended up producing this incredible song, which to this day is one of my favorite songs ever called *Captain*. The lyrics sing, "Through waters uncharted, my soul will embark. I'll follow your voice straight into the dark, and if from the course you intend I depart, speak to the sails of my wandering heart." Ben was an unknown Irish college student at the time. A few on our team had told me not to give him false hope by listening to his "green" songs, but that night I saw how the puzzle pieces could fit together. I watched a humble, graciously offered song fit perfectly into the life of our team and our church. It brought a freshness in our quest for God and provided a new worship vocabulary.

BE GENEROUS WITH YOUR PRAISE IN PUBLIC.

Specific, timely praise helps to create a culture that is generous in nature and honoring of the right things. There is something beautiful about putting people on display for everyone to see for all the right reasons. In our NYC church, there's a crazy custom in each staff meeting to put people "on front street;" they call out something great about each other that is meaningful, sincere and specific, and the whole team celebrates that person in that moment. In our current climate, Instagram and Facebook are perfect forums for telling good stories of people's sacrifice, service and surrender. We cultivate culture. We get to choose what we talk about and who we talk about, and I believe there is real Biblical wisdom in honoring all the parts—the seen and the unseen.

Some of the most significant worship leaders you'll ever meet today will never stand on a stage in front of a congregation; they run projector graphics from the back of the room, or wrap cables at the end of worship or sit behind lighting desks. These are people who understand that whatever they find to do, if they do it with their whole heart and unto the Lord, then it is the sweetest form of worship (see Colossians 3:23). Our Communications Director, Jay Argaet, is possibly one of the greatest evangelists you will ever meet. He is passionate about winning the lost by creating campaigns where people are confronted by the incredible love of Jesus. Each Easter, he sky writes " † = ♥ " across major cities in Australia; he sees his role as ensuring that as much as it is within his power, none will perish without having been given the opportunity to hear the Good News of Jesus. He is talented and clever, but most of all he loves Jesus and his church, and it is contagious. His whole team ends up reflecting his passion. He's quick to give credit; I've seen the people around him continue to generate innovative, beautiful work as it's valued and esteemed.

One thing I love about the team I lead is that passivity is gone. They don't wait for someone to tell them they have done well. They go and seek out others to praise. They think generationally and look for the twelve-year-olds timidly starting out on the worship team to reach their hands out to help and speak life over them. They talk about the God potential that resides within our willingness to serve; in doing this they cause the Church to be robust and sustainable. We have struck gold, and the mine is rich. All it took was a little extravagance, a lot of risk and putting ourselves outside of our comfort zones. It is absolutely, positively beautiful.

PROMPT: Our senior pastor always says, "If you want to change culture, you never do it by talking about it. You do it by being what you want to see." I've come to know that this is the absolute truth when it comes to encouragement and leadership. Many people want to be encouraged—they wait desperately for someone to recognize something in them or to notice what they do; if only they would take the initiative. If you want to change the culture around you, whether it's your church, your small group, your workplace or your family, take the initiative. Ask the Holy Spirit to give you eyes to see the people around you the way that He does. Then, get vocal with the things you're seeing. Pick up a pen, write a card. Approach someone on your team and compliment them from a place of encouragement and sincerity. You are powerful and capable of confident, extravagant leadership.

TOOL № 3 : THE GRATITUDE TOOL

let gratitude change you

As a community we have learned the power of gratitude and how it transforms our inner world. For the past decade, we've practiced using the Honesty Tool alongside the Gratitude Tool. Commitment to both balances our emotional worlds and strengthens our identity as the Father's beloved. As we begin to uproot false beliefs through honesty with God, it is important to rebuild new belief systems through receiving God's perspective and practicing thankfulness toward Him. Engaging gratitude in simple moments leads us to discover God's generosity and how He is fighting for our breakthrough.

For every Honesty Tool, we want to encourage you to practice a Gratitude Tool. This rhythm gets our eyes off our personal drama, and creates space for us to shape the new belief systems that transform our lives. Gratitude empowers us to move beyond negative beliefs like, *I am alone* or *It's all up to me* to become people who build up powerful core beliefs like, *I am covered* and *I am loved.*

"Enter with the password: 'Thank you!' Make yourselves at home, talking praise. Thank Him. Worship Him. For God is sheer beauty, all-generous in love, loyal always and ever." Psalms 100:4-5, MSG

STOP AND REFLECT

Identify a simple moment when you felt positively affected. This moment is not limited to a feeling of joy, it can include a range of feelings like being loved, seen, heard, respected or even experiencing relief from a stressful situation. It can be simple. The Father is constantly offering us beautiful truths even in the smallest moments.

"Moreover, we have seen with our own eyes and can testify to the truth that Father God has sent his Son to be the Savior of the world. Those who give thanks that Jesus is the Son of God live in God, and God lives in them. We have come into an intimate experience with God's love, and we trust in the love he has for us." I John 4:14-16, TPT

EXPRESS YOUR GRATITUDE

Write out an honest prayer of gratitude in response to the situation and let it affect you! Take time to recall your thoughts and feelings and take note of how you were acting. Include these things in your response. Engage gratitude toward God and any other person involved. God gives us moments to reinforce powerful belief systems in our hearts. Choosing gratitude opens our eyes to fully receive these gifts!

"Give thanks to the Lord, for he is good; his love endures forever."
Psalms 107:1, NIV

MAKE CONNECTIONS

After completing your thankful prayer, take a moment and read what you wrote and reflect. Let the kindness of God and others wash over you. Underline and create a list of the powerful thoughts and conclusions you made in your prayer.

"Every good and perfect gift is from above, coming down from the Father of the heavenly lights..." James 1:17, NIV

LISTEN & RECEIVE

After completing your list of powerful conclusions, take a breath and invite the Father to speak to you. Invite Him to affirm what he was communicating to you through this specific situation. God is excited to speak to you and build you up. He is fighting for your wholeness and knows the truth you need to receive.

"My sheep hear my voice, and I know them, and they follow me." John 10:27, ESV

TOOL Nº 3 : THE GRATITUDE TOOL

here's my example,

by JONATHAN HELSER

This tool has changed my life. It can be so easy to hurry through life and rush past the moments where God is engineering circumstances to confirm our belovedness. This tool has helped me to slow down and allow God's love to deeply transform me. A few years ago, Melissa and I did a week long worship tour across Europe. We played in six cities over seven days. It was a whirlwind trip full of a lot of incredible moments, but it was also very taxing for Melissa because of the chronic illness she has. Also, several of our flights were canceled on the way to Europe, which complicated our plans. But on the last day of our trip, we had some extraordinary favor and our flights were rerouted through Paris, so we had an extra day off in that beautiful city. On top of that, we were upgraded to first class on our flight back home. I decided to do a gratitude tool while we flew over the Atlantic and really let this moment affect me.

1 STOP AND REFLECT

Father, thank you for surprising Melissa and I with a day in Paris and an upgraded flight home.

2 EXPRESS YOUR GRATITUDE

Father, thank you so much for the last week in Europe and this day in Paris. My heart is overflowing with gratitude to you. I love that you chose to close this journey with a first class upgrade for our flight home. At this moment I feel so seen and known by you. My heart feels the beautiful weight of your faithfulness like the brilliance of the sun on a day at the seaside. Your goodness is washing me of all the lies and pressure fear puts on my shoulders. You truly are a father who loves to fulfill the desires of my heart. I lean back into your pursuit of me and I give you my trust. Lord, help me stay focused on you in the days ahead. I run to you in this moment of favor and I let my roots reach deeper into the reality of who you are and what you think of me. Thank you for being such a good Father and constantly doing more than I could dream.

3 MAKE CONNECTIONS

- I am seen by God and He knows my heart.
- God loves to fill the desires of my heart.
- God's goodness destroys lies and fears.
- I am the Father's beloved son.
- God does more than I could dream.

4 LISTEN & RECEIVE

Jonathan David, it is my joy as a Father to give you the desires of your heart. I know that you have been in the fire with Melissa's health and my heart feels the pain more than you could ever know.

Breathe me in son. I am with you right now. You sing the words, "Your faithfulness will never let me down." Now, it's time to believe those words and walk in the confidence that you will see my goodness in everything. I love being apart of every detail in your life. I am your shepherd and your provider. Don't let your heart be overwhelmed with what is impossible in your strength. Rather, let your heart be filled with astonishment that nothing is impossible for me. Let your soul be swept away with the reality that my faithfulness will never let you down.

by JESSIE MILLER
photograph by MORGAN CAMPBELL

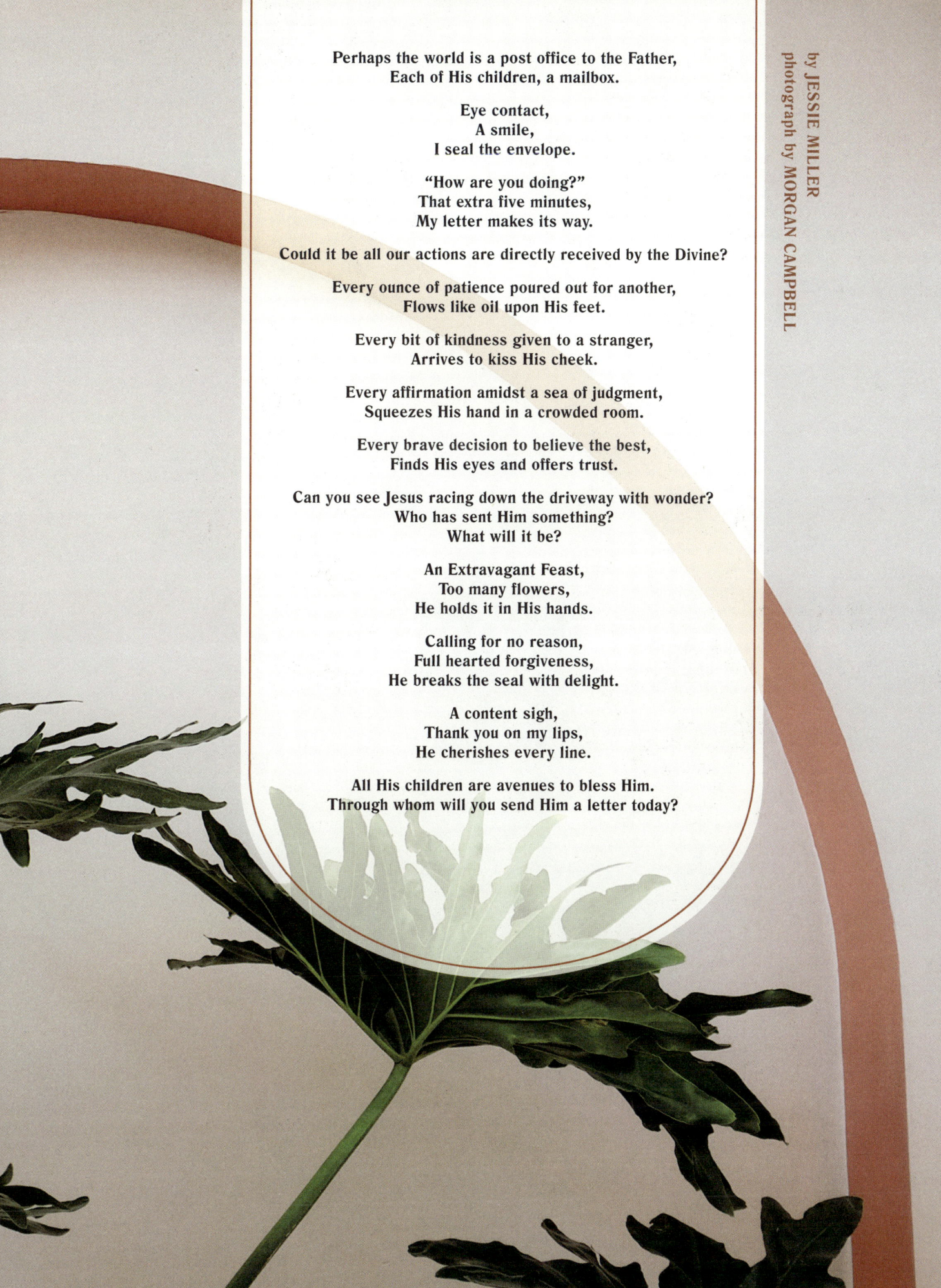

Perhaps the world is a post office to the Father,
Each of His children, a mailbox.

Eye contact,
A smile,
I seal the envelope.

"How are you doing?"
That extra five minutes,
My letter makes its way.

Could it be all our actions are directly received by the Divine?

Every ounce of patience poured out for another,
Flows like oil upon His feet.

Every bit of kindness given to a stranger,
Arrives to kiss His cheek.

Every affirmation amidst a sea of judgment,
Squeezes His hand in a crowded room.

Every brave decision to believe the best,
Finds His eyes and offers trust.

Can you see Jesus racing down the driveway with wonder?
Who has sent Him something?
What will it be?

An Extravagant Feast,
Too many flowers,
He holds it in His hands.

Calling for no reason,
Full hearted forgiveness,
He breaks the seal with delight.

A content sigh,
Thank you on my lips,
He cherishes every line.

All His children are avenues to bless Him.
Through whom will you send Him a letter today?

An Interview with Kamran Yaraei

WHEN GOD COMES TO COOK

HOW ONE MAN'S LOVE FOR FOOD HAS SHAPED A COMMUNITY WITH GOD'S KINDNESS

by Allie Sampson and Justina Stevens
photography by Morgan Campbell

Kamran Yaraei is a former Shiite Muslim from Iran

who came to America in 1997 and through a series of miraculous events came to know Jesus as his Lord, Savior and Friend. As an author and teacher, Kamran speaks globally from his heart-connection with God. He and his wife, Suzy, live in the mountains of western North Carolina. Kamran has a high value for hospitality and preparing meals, and he frequently finds God speaking to him in the kitchen. His relationship with the Father is marked with a keen sensitivity and his simple rhythms of finding God in the mundane are powerful. We spent a summer's afternoon sitting down with Kamran in his peach orchard to hear more of his story and how he stays connected to God and others. As you read about his life, may you be filled with inspiration to make space for the Father in the simple moments of your day.

HOW WOULD YOU DESCRIBE YOUR LIFE MESSAGE?

I would say just to really love God, to walk with Him and be His friend. Every now and then I check in and ask myself, *Kamran, when you really look deep down inside, what do you want to be? Who are you? What would really make you come alive?"* And the answer always is to be His friend.

WHEN DID YOU FIRST FEEL FASCINATED BY GOD?

I was working in my dad's supermarket when I was twelve years old. We lived in a small city in Iran, but my dad's was the best supermarket in town. All the Muslim religious leaders (the Imam) would come in to shop for groceries and I would ask them questions about God. As I got older, the questions became more serious. I'd ask, "How can I become a friend of God?" And to the Imam, that question was arrogant for a small boy to ask; they would tell my dad that I was "out there." They'd say, "He asks questions that he shouldn't." I was fascinated, not because I read anything, but because God was putting those questions in my heart. I remember I would sit at my dad's supermarket door, looking outside and waiting for a man of God to walk in—we called them "dervish" like Muslim mystics—but I never found anybody to give me the answers I longed for. Dervish were a myth; people would talk about them, and we heard all these stories about them. Like Rumi, he was a thirteenth century Persian poet and Sufi mystic. Rumi was the closest thing for me to all these ideas I had in my mind about a friend of God. Knowing he existed made me think my questions weren't crazy. I thought, *If Rumi talked about the things of God, I want to know about them too.*

HOW DID YOU MEET JESUS?

The first time I met Jesus was in Cyprus, a neighbor island country close to Iran. At thirty years old I was sick and tired of religion, Islam and even pursuing Allah. Just imagine: since I was twelve, I'd been sitting at my dad's store looking for someone to come give me answers to my spiritual questions. And now eighteen years later, I had a broken heart and wanted to run away to America to get away from Iran, Allah, everything. All my dreams were shattered.

Getting to the US wasn't an easy task, because Iranians had to get a visa and the US government really didn't even let Iranians enter the country. Iran didn't even have an American Embassy; I had to travel to the one in Cyprus. I had one of my close friends get me an appointment to a travel agency, and they got me an appointment at the American Embassy. So, the night I got to my hotel in Cyprus, I was sitting there in the lobby with nothing to do since my visa appointment wasn't until the next day. I didn't have anywhere to go, plus I didn't even speak the Turkish or Greek languages. I was so confused about my life. Out of the corner of my eye I saw a Bible in Farsi, my native language. I took the Bible to my hotel room and opened this book for the first time in my life. The story I read was so sweet; I kept thinking, *Why is this story so soothing?* Because the Quran (holy book of Islam) was never soothing to me growing up, I was captivated with this Bible. While I read, something supernatural began to happen. Every time I would get to the word 'Jesus Christ,' the ink would literally jump off the page in front of my very eyes and float to the ceiling very slowly, and then come and land back onto the page. I kept reading, and this happened three or four times!

The last time it happened I looked up, and the Lord was standing there before me. He was wearing a turban on his head like a Middle Eastern man; the ceiling expanded way higher than my actual room. I'd never seen this man before, but my whole body knew, *Oh this is Jesus Christ, the prophet to Christians.* Jesus didn't correct me, "Oh hey, I'm not a prophet. I'm the Son of God." He didn't say anything for a while, and then He said to me in Farsi, "I will help you go to the United States." I looked in my heart and thought, *Can I pray to this Jesus? He's a prophet to Christians. I am a Muslim.* Suddenly I got so passionate and angry and said, "Jesus, no other prophets can help me! If you can, please do." I went to the embassy the next day, and they handed me my visa. Just like that. That was the first time I met Jesus. I wasn't even thinking about Jesus; I wasn't pursuing Him at all. Even so, He got me in the place He wanted me to be. After all those years, He appeared to me and didn't even say who He was.

WHERE DO YOU FIND GOD THE MOST? HOW DO YOU ENGAGE INTIMACY WITH GOD?

Definitely through food. One day I was frying an egg. I was very hungry, not even thinking of anything spiritual. I used to use a lot of oil when I fried my eggs. I liked to get the oil really hot then drop the egg in the pan to hear the sizzling sound it makes. I was listening to the sizzle that morning, and it made me think of my mom—she used to cook her eggs like that. I felt God standing next to me in that moment. He said, "Do you hear that?" I asked, "What?" And He said, "Do you *hear* that? That is me." I paused everything, thinking He was joking with me. I told Him, "You're just tricking me. How is that sound you?" He replied, "Where there is sound, there is life. And where there is life, I am there." Still I didn't get it. He explained, "I want you to find me when I come to you in the sound of a frying egg." That day changed my life; it wasn't about the food anymore. It was about awareness of God— He could manifest through my food at any moment. For me, cooking food is an invitation for God. If He could manifest through cloud or fire in the Bible, He can surely manifest through my omelette.

Being from Iran, food and hospitality are huge in our culture; it's that way even in the Bible. I think that's why Jesus told me I need to cook for people with my hands, because cooking is a concept I understand. I feel the need to buy and cook great meat—good lamb, good beef. I can feel God when I do that. Mixing the meat, marinating it—it's an all day process that I love. Putting a meal in front of people and them saying, "We've never tasted anything like this!"— it's the Father revealing Himself to people without them knowing it's Him. Some people can only find the Father like in the Old Testament, when He comes with prosperity. When Jesus came to Earth, some people couldn't find Him because He was in a different form. And now that we have the Holy Spirit today, it's like, *Good luck finding Him!* It can be tough for people to find Him, see Him. I've found God in a lot of pain and agony, in tears, in difficulty and problems. And I can also find Him in the good things: when I plant a tree in my orchard, when I walk around nature with Suzy, when I make my favorite food for friends, even when I sit in front of the TV. These are all times I engage intimacy with God; I can feel Him wanting to walk with me, talk with me.

HOW HAVE YOU TAKEN THIS CONNECTION WITH GOD AND CREATED CONNECTIONS WITH OTHERS?

The Lord asked me once, "If you had a meeting at your house, what would you like to do?" I told Him that I would love to cook for people. He said, "Cook for them with your own hands, and when they finish eating, bless them." We started having people in our home regularly, and every time we would eat a meal we would bless them like our lives depended on it! We loved it. We hosted those meetings for two years before we ran out of space for all the people. "Now what do we do, God?" He answered, "Take it to the people. Take it to the city." We planted our meetings like a seed at a local coffee shop in our town, and the numbers of people who would come and eat grew and grew. People loved my homemade ground beef and chicken kebabs with saffron. Two and a half years in, and people still like it. I figure, you can preach about God or you can cook for them. To me it's the same. I'm not embarrassed to say that it is actually Jesus serving the people, not me. I think of Jean Valjean from Victor Hugo's *Les Misérables*—this hardened convict didn't have a change of heart by hearing a preacher talk about God's love; instead, he changed and transformed with one shocking act of kindness. Why don't we open a new portal for people to be astonished by God's love and hospitality?

WHAT WOULD YOUR ADVICE BE FOR SOMEONE WHO WANTS TO CREATE A PLACE OF CONNECTION BUT DOESN'T KNOW WHERE TO START?

Cooking is a part of my heritage, my family—it's a passion of mine. God asked me what I would use to connect with others around me, so naturally I responded with an idea to share good food. But that's not for everyone. If God were to ask you what you could use to create a space to know other people, what could it be? Gardening? Music? God asks good questions; don't be afraid to answer honestly from the depths of who you are.

I WAS SITTING ON A PLANE NEXT TO A GUY WHO SMELLED LIKE HE HAD JUST DINED AT A KOREAN BBQ RESTAURANT— THE SMELL OF GARLIC AND ONIONS HITTING ME—AND WHO MUST HAVE JUST DRANK A WHOLE LIQUOR STORE FULL OF ALCOHOL; OR SO HIS BREATH TOLD ME AS HE SNORED LOUDLY IN MY DIRECTION.

BECAUSE

by SHAWN BOLZ

I was on a red-eye flight in the middle of the night, and I had meetings in the morning. I realized I wasn't going to be able to sleep with my seatmate next to me, so I just surrendered, got up and said under my breath, "God, here I am. I am either going to get real cranky and whiny, or I am going to press into you to make the most of this time."

I walked to the bathroom, and the flight attendant there said to me, "I am so sorry about that guy sleeping next to you. We have no other seats. How are you able to stand it?" I laughed and told her that I was a Christian and that I was going to turn this into a time of praying for the people I loved. I asked her if there was anything she needed prayer for. "No, not really," she started. Then she said, "Well, you can pray for my son." Instead of jumping right to pray, I tried to be present and engage the love she had for him: *Why did he need prayer? Was he okay?* I thought of I Corinthians 2:10, "The Spirit, not content to flit around on the surface, dives into the depths of God, and brings out what God planned all along. Who ever knows what you're thinking and planning except you yourself? The same with God—except that he not only knows what he's thinking, but he lets us in on it" (MSG). I began to ask God for His thoughts for this woman's son, and a thought dropped in my heart just like that Scripture said; it was like God's perceptions overlapped mine. Maybe I was tired enough to not be guarded in my over-analytical nature, or just maybe His compassion was moving me. I had to ask her: "Is your son's name Steve?"

She was taken aback. "Do you know him?" I was so surprised that God showed me his name that I didn't know what to do except to tell her the rest of the thought I had for Steve. "Is he dating a girl? And their relationship has been pretty toxic?" "Yes, but how do you know this? Are you friends with him?" She had no context for what was happening. "I am a Christian, like I said, and right when you asked me to pray for your son I had a spiritual thought that I think is from God. He showed me your son by name and that the toxic relationship he is in is ending while we are on this plane. You are going to have your son back by the time we land. God wants you to be gentle with him because his heart is broken. God wants to help him dream about his career again, which was suppressed by this relationship." She was in shock, "I can't believe this! I mean, I have been praying and praying for them to break up. She literally stole his life away from him. I so hope this really is God." "Well, there's one way to find out," I said. "When we land he will tell you if they are together or not. If they are not, call me." I gave her my cell phone number. She hugged me and thanked me. I knew she felt loved and respected from what I shared, and I went back to my seat grateful.

Although I often come across as an extrovert, I am a hopeless introvert; one of the miracles of this moment was that God gave me love as a context to talk to this woman. I thought, *If I had a kid who was in danger relationally, I would be desperate to hear from God. I would be desperate for advice or help.* This compassion compelled me before I could rationalize fear, unbelief or take out the mystery of the moment by over-analyzing the experience. Love does that; it causes you to look past yourself and see others.

OF LOVE

It causes you to be the normal you. Love actually causes you to be the most connected version of yourself because you are not performing. You are vulnerable. It causes you to forget that you can't do something. People move whole cars to save the lives of others trapped under them with the power of compassion. I have found my own limitations lift as I allow my heart to empathize and fill up for someone else. Whether for a homeless person whom I normally wouldn't want to stop for, or for a stranger at a grocery store while I have my toddlers and am busy, love causes me to connect in a way that is outside of my normal.

So, what happened with the flight attendant who I normally would've ignored? She called me and told me, "I have my son back. Now, how did God show this to you, and what religion are you? We want to talk to you about this!" I was able to have a conversation with her because love opened a door, a door usually only opened in trusted relationships—like a therapist, best friend or a pastor. Love gave context that bridged the gap of our lack of relationship; it opened their family to truly understand Jesus and Christianity, which they wholeheartedly accepted!

PROMPT:

I want to encourage you to take your limitations out of the equation of love. You never know what you are capable of when you allow your heart to be moved by the Lord. Today you might be an introvert, but tomorrow you might be the life of the party because of love. Today you might not like to talk to certain types of people, but tomorrow he or she might be the sole person on your radar. Take a few minutes to be still for some listening prayer. Ask God to show you someone, preferably someone you don't know, you get to love this week. Write down what you feel from God's heart. This will change the way you are present, the way you love and the way you respond to this love with faith on behalf of his or her need.

EXTRAVAGANCE

TEACHING A GENERATION EXTRAVAGANCE

by JONATHAN HELSER

photography by the CAGELESS BIRDS

I THINK ONE OF THE MOST INSPIRING AND CHALLENGING CHARGES FOUND IN THE SCRIPTURES FOR MEN IS IN THE BOOK OF EPHESIANS, WHEN HUSBANDS ARE INSTRUCTED TO, "LOVE YOUR WIVES, JUST AS CHRIST LOVED THE CHURCH AND GAVE HIMSELF UP FOR HER" (EPHESIANS 5:25, NIV). What an extravagant standard of love husbands are summoned to. The greatest act of love in history was when Christ fully gave His body and soul on a cross for His Bride. When I read these words from Ephesians, they initiate something deep inside of me to become a servant, a warrior and a wholehearted lover like Jesus. I can remember being a little boy and watching the way my father adored my mother. This awakened a desire in me from a young age to be a husband one day and to love my bride with that kind of love. I am currently two decades into marriage and I am still on the quest to fulfill this commission to love like Jesus.

Just as I was influenced by my parents' marriage, I now have the privilege of inspiring the students that come through our schools. Our discipleship school is made up of students ranging from twenty to thirty years old. They come to our land from all over the world. We tell our students that during the school, "More will be caught than will be taught." Our school is life-on-life discipleship and because our students live on the land with us, they get to watch us live our lives, day in and day out. This has a profound impact on them, especially in regards to family and marriage. So many in this generation have come from broken homes and have wrestled with their sexuality. They have such a deep need to be initiated. They are longing for someone ahead of them in life to teach them and prepare them for what's ahead. When our students watch the way Melissa and I interact as a husband and a wife and when they see the way that we parent our children, it has a deep effect on them. The way we show each other affection or the way we work through conflicts—our students are watching and learning from all of these moments. Even the simplicity of having the students in our home and sitting around our table for a meal speaks volumes to them on what marriage and family are meant to be.

During each of our schools, we split the guys and girls up into separate groups, and Melissa and I have the honor of sharing with them about sexuality, marriage and walking in the fullness of who God made them to be. We meet with them several times throughout the course of the school and it is incredible what God does. The highlight moment for me every year is the way we close these sessions. All the men of the school take an entire day to create an over-the-top, outrageous and extravagant meal for the ladies of the school. These nights have been affectionately called "Ladies' Night." Before we begin the preparations of hosting this lavish dinner for the ladies, I share with the guys the charge that we have been given as men to love with the extravagant love of Christ. As a leader, my goal for the night is to initiate the men into what it looks like to be a wholehearted servant-leader like Jesus. The staff and I work side-by-side with the students in the kitchen: joyfully planning, problem-solving and working hard to make the dream of this night a reality. I wish I could describe to you in words how incredible this night is. We pour our hearts into every facet of the night and spare no expense, from the decor, to the place settings, to the many courses of food we serve. Our desire is that the ladies feel like they are royalty and that they have been given reservations to one of the finest restaurants in the world. At the end of these nights, our guy students are physically exhausted, but their hearts are overflowing with joy and strength. They are standing up taller in their confidence, their eyes are glowing with pure light and their spirits are brimming over with the radiant hope of who they are created to be as men: Initiators. Servants. Lovers and warriors.

So many of our female students are in beautiful tears when they sit at the table that has been prepared for them. Many of them tell me that no one has ever done something so special for them. At the core of every woman is the need to be adored and fought for, and at the core of every man is the need to fight for something greater than himself. This is how we were created. That is the deeper essence and reason why these Ladies' Nights fulfill something so profound in the hearts of our students. By taking the time to set a table of extravagance, value and identity are restored and imparted into hearts.

That's why I love extravagance and why it has become a core pillar of our community. Ladies' Night is just one example of how we've worked this value into our lives. This idea may come across as quite epic and not attainable for your life, but this night grew from years of practicing extravagance in smaller ways, like writing a declaration of encouragement to a friend, hosting our staff for a special dinner or planning a surprise birthday party for someone on our team. I am enthralled with what happens when we dare to go the extra mile to communicate our love for another. When we choose to lay our lives down for another in big and little ways, we are loving like God does. One of the definitions of extravagance is, "A lack of restraint in use of resources."[10] God does not love us in moderation; He pours out His affection without restraint or limits. God speaks in the language of extravagance. He bankrupted Heaven and gave His one and only Son. He creates a new sunrise every morning and then paints the sky again each evening. He turns 180 gallons of water into wine at the end of a wedding feast. He does so many miracles that if they were all written down there would not be enough room in all the world to contain the books that would be written. When I breathe in the wonder of a God who loves with such generosity and abundance, it provokes me to love with His extravagant love.

PROMPT: Take some time to be still and ask the Holy Spirit to highlight a friend or a family member. Once you have chosen someone, ask the Lord to fill your heart with His love for that person. Take a few moments and turn that love into a prayer for them. Now, ask God for some creative ideas to express your love to that person in an extravagant way. It could be having them over for a meal and going the extra mile to cook them something very special. It could be buying them a special gift and writing them a declaration of how much you value them and what God says about them. God has so many creative ideas when it comes to expressing our love for one another. All we have to do is ask and then partner with Him. Let the Lord inspire and challenge you to fulfill the commission to, "Love each other just as much as I have loved you" (John 13:34, TPT).

GIFT of TEARS

by MOLLY SKAGGS
photograph by MORGAN CAMPBELL

Recently, a friend of mine reached out asking for time to connect with me. She is a friend of whom I am particularly fond—a fellow musician and kindred spirit who loves Jesus. She is someone I don't see often, but when I do, I am reminded of how much I wish I did. We carved out space in the midst of our mutual errand-running afternoon to chat on the phone. Immediately I noticed that her tone of voice wasn't as high and chipper as usual. Today, it was as friendly as ever, yet washed over with different shades of blue. Our conversation began as normal, the simple chatter of catching up on each other's lives. Slightly uneasy, but still very happy to hear her voice after such a long time, I said, "You mentioned in your text that you had something to share with me?" My friend then proceeded to tell me her most recent health diagnosis. Her doctors told her she had an autoimmune disease that would progressively limit normal functioning in her hands and feet, ultimately locking up her entire body. "Molly," she said, "They told me I would begin to lose my ability to play music and that I should start looking for a different career."

A breathless moment passed between us. All of a sudden, I felt a deep agonizing pain as if I had been punched hard right in my soul. I broke into a million tiny pieces inside my car, "I am so sorry." Memories of her music, her glorious sound began to flood my mind and ring in my ears. This sickness was with her now, threatening to take these beautiful parts of her away from all of us, like snuffing out a candle. I couldn't hold back my tears and began to openly weep. All I could say was, "I'm so sorry," wishing that I could've been stronger for her somehow. All at once I heard it, the sound of her tears rolling down her freckled cheeks, the collected sadness in her voice, and for the next few minutes I wept with my friend. *If this were all happening to me*, a humble thought came, *if I was told I would start losing my ability to make music…Oh Father, what would I do? How would I feel?* The more she opened up and shared what was going on, more waves of empathy—sharp and warm—passed through my soul. I realized I was connecting to the pain and disappointment of her beautiful heart as if it were my own. "Is there anything I can do for you, friend?" I asked her wanting so desperately to do something, anything, to make it all better for her. She sighed deeply, "Honestly, this was the best thing you could've done. Thank you. I really just desire friends who see me and deeply care." No amount of positivity would magically heal her sick body or comfort her wounded soul. There was only One who could do that, and I believe with all my heart that He loves her more than I do and wants to heal her more than any of us want it.

Looking back now, I see that both she and Jesus invited me into a very sacred time in her story. In this moment of the deepest shared vulnerability, I witnessed firsthand how unafraid Jesus is to get as close as He can to our brokenness, sicknesses and pain. So often in the past, I would want to rescue and fix moments like this one, only to be humbly reminded I am powerless to change the circumstances. I am learning even more what it means to remain present in pain like God does, and that just when I feel I have nothing helpful or comforting to offer, He moves within my emotions and affirms that the giving of my own tears is sometimes the greatest thing I could do. I believe that being emotionally generous is a part of the very heart and nature of God. Our friends, families, co-workers and communities are suffering—oftentimes silently and in isolation out of fear that what they carry will be too much for the people in their lives. Love flows straight from God's heart and desires to always make its final destination where it hurts the most in us. Making ourselves vulnerable to the pain and suffering of those we care about and practicing empathy creates space for Love to do what it wants. Empathy is our ability to emotionally connect with another's joy, sadness, anger and pain as if it were our own. It is the willingness to allow all of our emotional faculties to be engulfed by those of another person, all for the goal of love and connection. If we are moved by compassion as Jesus was, we then move to action, even if that is being present, listening silently and letting our tears fall with the ones we love.

Prompt: Spend time with the Father in prayer, allowing Him to pinpoint someone in your life who may be suffering with physical or emotional pain. Let His heart affect you. Consider how you would feel if you were in their shoes. Jot your thoughts and feelings down in a journal. Remember, allowing yourself to feel someone's pain and connect with them is not the same as carrying the responsibility for their circumstance. That's God's job! From a place of empathy and compassion, let Him inspire you to take action. Perhaps you could share your love with them through a handwritten letter or a phone call. Maybe you could set up a time to meet with them personally and ask to hear their story. Let Love move you.

LOVING THE WORLD AROUND YOU

intro by ALLIE SAMPSON
photography by MELISSA HELSER

One of the most fascinating parts of the Gospels is how Jesus interacted with strangers. In the hustle of a crowd and the midst of daily life, He consistently moved toward people, prioritizing their hearts over the day's agenda or the cultural norms. His approach to the people around Him is inspiring, but applying it to our own lives—our own agendas, our own cultures, our own strangers—can be intimidating. It's hard to know where to start and how to reach out in a way that feels authentic and intuitive.

In this series, three of our Cageless Birds staff share moments when they've experienced the joy of the Lord in reaching out to strangers. As you read this series, we encourage you to remember that there is no way to perfectly orchestrate a moment with someone you don't know. But there is a way to practice values: a value for compassion, a value for kindness, a value for generosity. This can be quite simple. It can look like eye contact, learning someone's name or going out of your way to acknowledge them. May you be inspired to build your own value systems with the Lord and let Him fill you up with the possibilities of what could happen when you move toward those around you in love.

SLOW TO SPEAK

by ABIGAIL ROLLINS

I work in a very small, specific trade. Making high-quality leather goods by hand from start to finish is a beautiful process, though not a very common one. Many leather companies mass-produce their goods, and it's especially rare to find fellow artisans with a similar love and vision for the process. Maria is a brilliant and dedicated craftswoman, committed to creating leather bags that are timeless. She is far ahead of me in our craft, and when I saw her work online, I was inspired. I took a risk and reached out, hoping to make a business connection and to have the opportunity to ask an expert some of my lingering questions.

I was moved by her response. She invited me to her studio and offered to answer all of my questions. I'd come from a corporate background where business was built on keeping secrets of the trade. But here she was, full of generosity, offering to share all of her mistakes and triumphs openly with me. Conversation began to form organically, and soon, Maria started opening up more than her creative process. She began expressing the challenges of having to cover every aspect of her business—working extended hours to write, photograph and advertise in addition to making her products. All of this on top of working full time at a university. She opened up about how tired she was, and the lack of inspiration she was experiencing. "Why am I doing this? Does anyone know what I'm doing?"

As soon as Maria started sharing, I knew God was opening a door for me to encourage her. I felt empathy stirring in my heart. I remembered the exhaustion of late hours and the pressure I used to feel to do everything alone. An opportunity to encourage her was coming, I could feel it, but God kept telling me to wait. "Abby, let her talk. She needs to feel heard." I waited. I listened. The more she shared, the more connection built. Eventually there was a pause, and I felt permission to speak in. I spoke affirmation, shared how deeply I'd been affected by her work and encouraged her to keep going.

Tears filled her eyes. A smile of gratitude swept over her face. "Thank you for saying that. I'm so glad you came."

I went to Maria's studio that day to learn from her. I was drawn to her business by the sense of understanding I felt through her work, and when I arrived, understanding was the gift that she received from the Lord through simple encouragement. Jesus wanted to validate her heart and affirm the places where she was taking a big risk professionally, financially and practically. The Lord wanted to remind Maria that she wasn't alone and that the work of her hands wasn't fruitless. He wanted to give the same gift to me.

Knowing how and when to practice empathy, especially in business relationships, can seem tricky but I've found that the key is sensitivity to the Holy Spirit. This simple moment could've played out really differently. When Maria began to share, instead of giving into anxiety or over-analyzing myself and the situation, I just kept listening for the heart of the Father. *What do you want to say, Holy Spirit? Oh, I remember exactly how that feels. Where are the places you want to encourage her today?* So much can happen when I am quick to listen and slow to speak.

WITH KINDNESS
by PHYLLIS UNKEFER

I really enjoy outgoing people. The kind who make friends with everyone they meet. I would not say, however, that I was one of them. It's not for a lack of kindness—I notice people and I genuinely care about them—but I'm initially on the quiet side, a bit more reserved. It turned out, Roger was too.

Roger is an older gentleman, slender, with pure white hair. He drives a UPS truck and when it pulls up to our shipping office door, we like to announce it, "Look, Roger's here!" Two of my friends and I spend our mornings packaging orders for our online store—books, leather journals, a ceramic mug or two. Every day, mail carriers stop by our office to drop off packages. When Roger first took over the delivery route, he was not quite as friendly as our previous UPS deliverer. He stayed focused on his job and often seemed pretty tense. I sensed that he wasn't in love with his work and figured it was hard to be alone all day. For weeks we only exchanged hellos, until one morning he paused to say, "By the way, what's your name?" I said, "Phyllis. What's yours?" "Hi Phyllis, I'm Roger." We both smiled before he strode back out. I delighted over the moment with my shipping teammates, and that's when we decided to befriend him.

It took consistency. We always greeted Roger by name, smiled and asked how he was. When I saw his truck, I'd gear myself up (the way we reserved people do) to intentionally make small talk. And eventually, he loosened up. He learned our names. From time to time, he asked what music we were listening to. In response to "How are you?" he'd playfully reply, "Tickled to be here." It's funny how affection grows. One day, I risked awkwardness and asked Roger when his birthday was. He paused, raised his eyebrows, but then offered, "April 21st."

So that April, we planned a party. A happy birthday sign. Baked cookies. And a cup of coffee. It wasn't just the shipping team and I; others from the admin department joined in. When we saw him in the driveway, we took on the demeanor of giddy ten-year-olds, turned off the lights and waited. But we didn't exactly foresee this unraveling of events: His first step through the door. Our jump and excited shout. The lights flashing on. More people in the room than usual. We yelled, "Happy birthday!" and his whole body went tense. His face dropped. He said an abrupt, "Thank you," grabbed a singular cookie and swiftly returned to his truck. We'd effectively terrified him. You can imagine how we felt—devastated is too strong a word, but somewhere slightly on the verge.

Days passed before another UPS delivery came, enough time to consider every way we would've revised the party and dramatically wonder if he hated us now. We were afraid we had ruined our efforts to befriend him. No one happened to be in the office the next time he stopped by. And we're so used to mail piling onto our shipping table, that we could have overlooked one envelope. I saw it first. Tore it open and found this written inside: "Girls, thank you very much for my birthday party! You girls are the highlight of my day with your bright smiles and kind hearts. Hope you like chocolate. These are my favorites. - Roger." Three chocolate bars were stacked under the card. As I read, relief came, mixed with delight.

We're planning another birthday party for Roger this year. Something low-key and involving his favorite dessert. He chats with us more than ever; we've learned that he loves hunting and musical instruments. And he regularly brings us chocolate. Our small attempts at connection, even the ones that appear to fall horrendously flat, go further than we realize. They can become the steady brightening of someone's day, and the gradual lifting of a heart. They can fill the ordinary spaces of life with God's nature: kindness.

INVESTING IN ANOTHER
by ROSEMARY SKAGGS

When Luke and I got married, we were excited about setting a value for generosity in our family. One of the small ways we both felt like we could practice being generous was in tipping our waiters and waitresses extravagantly whenever we went out to eat. This was something that hit home for me because I worked as a waitress and a barista for several years of my life before going into full-time ministry. The long hours on your feet, the constant interactions with people for better or for worse, making sure everyone is happy and has what they need—it can be a tough job!

One place in particular where we have seen the fruit of this value play out is at our favorite date night spot: a cozy, modern pizza place with a friendly vibe. Whenever we would eat there, it just so happened that the same guy would wait on us. Each time we would be intentional to make eye contact with him, smile and ask him how he was doing, thank him for serving us and leave a generous tip—oftentimes with a little thank you note written on the receipt.

He was very quiet in the beginning. We'd try to make conversation, but he wouldn't stick around long. He was hesitant to say our names and wouldn't greet us, but we could tell that it wasn't because he was unfriendly. We weren't offended by his distance and felt compassion for him. God was moving our hearts. We cared about him. Despite the reserved response we'd sometimes get, we made a point to ask him simple questions, making space for him to connect with us if he wanted to.

Over time, we began to notice him opening up to us. He was smiling and talking to us more and more, and he would often express that we were his favorite customers and the nicest people he'd ever waited on. Eventually he opened up to us about some of his life dreams, particularly one about starting a craft coffee shop in town. Luke and I both encouraged him, telling him we believed in him and that he was totally capable. Later, during one of his last shifts we felt prompted to give him more than our usual tip, and wrote a little note saying that this small contribution was to go toward his dream of pursuing his own business, and again that we believed in him.

It's been a long time since we've seen him. He could be passionately pursuing his dream of starting a craft coffee business now or he could not be. Regardless, I know that Luke and I saying yes to the Father's invitation of being generous in the small things opened up the door for big things to happen inside of his heart and our hearts. I know that our repeated generosity sent a continuous message to him: You matter. You're valuable.

I used to believe that simple gestures like this were insignificant; it didn't measure up to the larger-than-life picture of generosity I had in my head. But these moments are where I've learned that generosity is actually practical and completely doable. Watching the simple generosity we practiced affect someone we hardly knew led me to believe that generosity, simple or grand, is always significant and always worth it.

TO THE ENDS OF THE EARTH

by MATT PETERSON
photography by BEN ROBERTS

YEARS AGO, I WAS UNSURE OF WHAT I COULD DO TO IMPACT THE WORLD, in addition to loving my growing family, giving what I could financially and serving in my church. I had a strong desire to bring the Gospel to untouched countries, but didn't know how to start. One evening over a meal with my friend, Tim, a spark and a question set in motion something I never expected. Tim began excitedly sharing how God had given him an idea; it was a business idea that began with roasting coffee in the US and then using the profits to set slaves free in Nepal—and it was working. People who had been slaves for generations were purchased for as little as eight dollars apiece. They were freed, given land, food and the Gospel. They were becoming successful farmers, and their lives had been forever changed. Hearing Tim's stories violently stirred my heart as uncontrollable tears came out of me, along with a desire to do something creatively inspired. Later, while alone, I asked God a dangerous question: "Since you are the Creator of all things and all creative ideas flow from you, would you give me one idea that would change the lives of many people?"

Nothing came at first. Then, several months later an idea popped in my mind that started me on a journey of discovery to help provide clean drinking water for people suffering in developing nations. As I pursued the idea, researched, prayed and developed a concept for implementation, God led me to visit Africa. The last day that I was in Tanzania, I asked God if He wanted me to eventually work there. Moments after asking that question, a young boy driving cattle walked over to me and in perfect English said, "Give me water." I was shocked—the very thing God had placed upon my heart to help give! I returned to the US with a nation to help and shared the concept of giving water to the thirsty of Africa in a church meeting. After the meeting, a man named Dr. Chacha approached me and told me that his sister had died of a waterborne disease (one of many waterborne diseases which kill nearly 2,000 people daily, mostly children). He asked me if I could help him give water to his own people living in a remote area in—of all places—Tanzania! With the help of some compassionate volunteers who joined with me, we started a non-profit organization called Hydrating Humanity and went to Tanzania to begin.

Today, Hydrating Humanity is thriving and transforming areas in Africa; it's the glorious idea of God brought to life in a way that's more than I could've imagined! Our team helps provide clean drinking water and essential hygiene education to some of the 700 million people on the planet who have never tasted clean water. We have the privilege of introducing every village and school we serve to Jesus, who gives living and eternal water to the soul. In the past fourteen years, we've helped over 280,000 people enjoy clean water daily in East Africa, and many more have been educated and made aware of God's love for them. We have seen a witch doctor turn to Jesus, we've witnessed warring clans stop fighting and become friends; we've seen school children who used to get sick from dirty water, live healthy lives and stay in school. We've watched many come to faith and some even get baptized in the water flowing from the protected sources. When I asked God my dangerous question, I never could've imagined that His response would result in thousands of lives being changed, both in the natural and the eternal.

This journey has been layered with connection. Connection on a local scale—my conversation with Tim, the little boy who asked for water, Dr. Chacha and his family in Tanzania, the men and women who joined our team and are making this dream a reality—is what made this vision possible. It is what's led to a much larger, global connection and partnerships around the world. The power of global connection is that I will never meet all of the people that my choices are affecting. I may never hear their stories, see transformation or know how they benefitted from the idea that God lent me. In most cases, I won't get to connect with them face-to-face. Global connection is about creating a pathway for the Lord to walk through and connect with a person. In local connection, I meet with people face-to-face, but connection on a macro scale requires a different kind of selflessness and trust that the Lord is going to connect with people through your idea and give them what they need.

Does your heart burn for global change, but you don't know where to start? Having a desire to make a global impact is a gift! Not everyone carries this same desire. If you have it in your heart to help make a difference on a global scale, here are a couple of keys to help you in your journey:

ASK A DANGEROUS QUESTION

Asking God for an idea that will impact the world is risky—there's no guarantee that you'll get a safe answer. But, you may just get an invitation to an adventure greater than you could generate on your own. The dangerous question is a door to partnering with God. It's the starting point for bringing Heaven to the earth and living water to the thirsty. The best place to start is to ask God for an idea. Remember, something may not come right away. That's okay! Keep asking, and trust that God sees the desire in your heart.

Jesus modeled a selfless lifestyle—a willingness to go, to give, to serve and lay His life down for others. This is the lifestyle that He brings His power through, and it is the lifestyle He calls us to live. It's also the most thrilling, rewarding lifestyle that exists, fulfilling the will of the Father and satisfying the desire within each of us to live with His purpose. The Father's will and the adventure that follows await our requests. Beyond our own imagination, the imagination of God—that sets captives free, provides water, food, clothing, healing, salvation and love to the suffering—is available to His children.

LEVERAGE YOUR PRIVILEGE

Along this journey, I've realized that the words of Jesus to "freely give what we have freely been given" means that we all are privileged, and every privilege has purpose attached to it. We are alive in this moment to leverage our privilege for the purpose of helping others, whether that's going to the ends of the earth or the end of the street in our neighborhood to shine brightly and give away what we have received. There are creative ideas awaiting our requests to receive them, and there are numerous lives just like ours that are thirsty for love and the transformative Spirit of God that you contain.

PROMPT: Simply ask the Father for a creative idea, an avenue or place for you to leverage the love, skills, resources and abilities that you have to help serve others. When you ask, believe that He will give you what you are requesting (see Luke 11:1-13 and James 1:6). Pay attention to the thoughts and ideas that come over the next several days, weeks and months; capture them! Respond by taking the next step with the Holy Spirit—be willing to serve, give, go or even to start something new. You will begin a journey of engaging with the will of the Father and touching the world in a way that will give life to others through you.

THE IMPROMPTU FEAST

by CHRIS MILLER
SHARING ENCOURAGEMENT IN THE MOMENT

"So speak encouraging words to one another. Build up hope so you'll all be together in this, no one left out, no one left behind. I know you're already doing this; just keep on doing it" (I Thessalonians 5:11, MSG).

Community has to be more than good food and a beautiful table. In a time when it's easier and far more common to tear others down with sarcasm and cynical judgment, genuine encouragement is a powerful tool to breathe courage into relationships. Encouragement binds a team together, reinforces trust and fills the heart with confidence.

Encouragement and declarations are a life-giving rhythm of our community. We believe that God is eternally writing incredible stories on the pages of our lives. Over the last several years, our ministry has grown from schools and internships into a thriving community of friends and staff with beautiful marriages and families. In the midst of building projects, release dates and leading schools, we have to actively practice seeing one another and celebrating the image of God in each of our lives.

Recently, we sat down for a weekly planning meeting with our visual department. From the start, one of our core leaders expressed that she felt tired and discouraged by recent events. Intuitively, we shifted into a time of encouraging her—spontaneously highlighting places she had impacted us and championing the places we saw Jesus in her. The atmosphere of the room shifted and we decided to encourage the rest of the team. This only took fifteen minutes, but the result was tangible. Afterwards, we pressed into a meeting that was notably more joy-filled and productive.

Moments like this happen often in our workplace. We have found this to be a life-giving tool for both relational growth and productivity in a team. Years ago, one of our very first staff powerfully remarked, "Encouragement is the table where community feasts," and we took it to heart. We invite you to try it in your own community or family and let the Lord lead you into a new rhythm.

PROMPT: Can you imagine what it would be like if encouragement became normal in your circle of influence? How might the atmosphere change in your home? In your church body? At work? Who are the people you would like to practice this with? Pick a group of people you are doing life with. After choosing the group you want to try this with, take these four keys and give it a try. You can't fail, and chances are, it may well be something you want to practice throughout the year.

1. INVITE Invite your group into the heartbeat of the practice, and most importantly, invite the Holy Spirit into your session before you begin. Set the tone and share your expectations for how an encouragement session will look. To encourage someone is to breathe courage into their life, to give them the gift of being seen, known and loved for who they are. Identify and speak confidently to the places where you have experienced Jesus in this person. Has their kindness affected you? Has their patience in difficult situations inspired you? Has their generosity impacted you? The goal is to edify and build each other up! Make space for Him to fill the room with inspiration and confidence as you ask the Father to fill your hearts with language and pictures to encourage one another.

2. TIME IT Set a time boundary for each person to be encouraged. What is realistic? Don't underestimate what can be shared in five or seven minutes! Use a timer to ensure that each person in the group gets a turn.

3. RECORD IT Ask one volunteer to write down the spoken encouragement and/or digitally record it for each person. Encouragement isn't always accessible when we need it. Having a writing or recording to reflect back on gives us an opportunity to reconnect with our value at any point.

4. BE CLEAR Use clear and appropriate language for the relationship and avoid spiritual clichés. Let your encouragement be tangible, like, "You have the gift of hospitality; I always feel welcome in your home and have been deeply impacted by the generosity of your table," or, "I see the kindness of Jesus in the way you listen to others and make space for me whenever we speak." Speak to the truth and call to the greatness in one another. Have one person close each round of encouragement with a short prayer.

THE INTENTIONAL FEAST

by LINDSAY VANCE
SPENDING TIME CRAFTING YOUR WORDS AS GIFTS

Every August I sit at the long walnut table around a beautiful dinner with the Cageless Birds community, knowing that a downpour is coming, and if I stay here I am going to get drenched. Outside, the starry skies are clear, but inside, the air is thick with Heaven. It always rains on nights like this. My heart is open wide and I listen. It is my birthday, and my community has gathered to celebrate and honor the year I've just lived. They have sat in God's presence and asked Him to share His heart for me. I savor the sound as several of them take turns to stand and confidently declare beauty and significance into my heart and future season. The gift of their words is a waterfall, soaking the worked soil of my soul.

It's a simple rhythm, yet the meaning these evenings hold is deep. We affectionately refer to this monthly celebration as "Birthday Night," and everyone in our community excitedly awaits the time when they will be celebrated. We all just as equally enjoy the reward of reading to our friends, watching their eyes fill with tears as we declare God's promises over their lives. Each word we share has been thoughtfully penned in partnership with the Holy Spirit, weighed on the scale of love. We recognize that we have full access to God's endless supply of thoughts over us (see Psalm 139:17), and when we speak them, the power of these words gives life.

For the rest of the year, these encouragements will resound in our inner worlds, marking us with belonging and purpose. We gather the pile of cards like our own personal stones of remembrance, each one evidence that God sees us, desires us and satisfies our hearts. At the end of every Birthday Night, it's much harder to deny that God's goodness is shining through every crack and crevice of our human frames. His thoughts over us are abundant, and as His friends, we are carriers of His thoughts toward the family that surrounds us.

PROMPT: While birthdays are a wonderful occasion to write encouragements, you don't have to wait until then to speak life over your friends.

1. NAME Think of one friend or leader who you would like to celebrate. Write their name at the top of a page in your journal. Ask God, "What encouraging truths are you speaking into this season of my friend's life?"

2. LISTEN God can speak to us in so many ways. Sometimes He comes through a mental picture or through a simple word or phrase. At other times, He may stir up thankfulness for this friend. If the words you hear or the pictures you see seem ordinary or silly, don't worry! Simply invite the Holy Spirit to speak into what you are seeing or hearing. Oftentimes, what seems simple to you speaks immense value into the heart of a friend. In the end, your words should feel full of joy and clarity, not confusion. Remember, the goal isn't to find the perfect prophetic word; it's simply to swim in the ocean of thoughts God has for those He loves and then choose one or two that you desire to give your friend.

3. CRAFT After you've listened for God's voice, begin to craft an encouraging word or declaration for your friend on a homemade card. Spend time searching for metaphors that express what you want to say. Try to come up with phrases that uniquely describe the way you feel rather than landing on the first sentence you can think of. You want your words to communicate, "You are special to me and to God, and I spent time crafting these words for you." Draw or paint a picture on the front of your card that expresses your words.

4. PRACTICE When you are finished, practice reading your declaration out loud. If you are smiling and feel full of joy to give these words as a gift, then you're ready! Prepare a special time you can share your word with your friend and using your voice, confidently declare the heavenly thoughts you've written for them.

photography by CHRIS MILLER

Each word has been thoughtfully penned in partnership with the Holy Spirit, weighed on the scale of love.

the art of NEIGHBOR —ING

An Interview with ADAM AND JULI COX

by JUSTINA STEVENS
Photograph *by* SYDNEE MELA

Adam and Juli Cox are dear friends of the Cageless Birds community and have been for decades. Adam, originally from North Carolina, has called Kansas City, Missouri home since 2000. Juli comes from the beautiful land of South Africa and she spent five years working with Youth With A Mission (YWAM) in England before making Kansas City her home. Adam married Juli in 2006 and they have three girls, Liliwyn, Selah and Noelle. They lead the Eldership and Core Team of Navah Church KC and also serve on the global and national oversight team for 24-7 Prayer Communities. They carry a passion to see people discover the reality of Jesus' love, walk in new identity as sons and daughters and live out the dreams of God in Kingdom family. Adam speaks all over the world about the Gospel of Jesus, including our very own 18 Inch Journey school at A Place for the Heart. Together, their dream is to teach people how to be the Church and not just come to a church building. By equipping people to live out rhythms of prayer, family and blessing others, they are learning how to love God and their neighbor on a daily basis. They've been walking this out in their neighborhood, Legacy East, for the last seventeen years. If you've ever wondered about what it means in the Bible to really "love your neighbor," pull up a chair and listen to the Cox's story of engaging their neighborhood when God answered their prayers in an unexpected way.

TELL US A BIT ABOUT HOW GOD TAUGHT YOU THE ART OF NEIGHBORING?

A: In Luke 10, one of the teachers of the law asks Jesus, "What should I do to inherit eternal life?" Jesus responds, "Well, you know the law. What does it say?" The man says, "Love the Lord your God with all your mind, soul and strength, and love your neighbor as yourself." Jesus says, "Good, do this and you'll live." But the man quickly says back, "But who is my neighbor?" And I think this is so classic, because the first thing the man does is try to find a loophole. We love knowing the right answer, but this is where it gets challenging. Essentially Jesus says, "How much desire for good and blessing and life do you want for yourself? Well, do that for your neighbor." We wonder if we can find a loophole too: *How can I keep this in the ethereal realm? Can I just keep that command as a generalized thing? Because I'll never have to really do what Jesus is saying if I don't know who my neighbor is.* Then Jesus tells this wild story about The Good Samaritan; He ends up saying, "The one who showed mercy, you go and do likewise." Jesus basically answers this whole question—Who is my neighbor?—by indicating, "Don't ask who your neighbor is. *Be* a neighbor." This core teaching shows us how to be a neighbor where we live. It comes down to the command: "Love God with all of your being, and love your neighbor as yourself" (see Luke 10:27).

For the first many years we lived in our neighborhood I wanted to do this, but I wanted my neighbor to be ethereal. Jesus challenged me with the thought, *What if neighboring was literal?* The art of neighboring comes down to: Do we know the actual people who live next door to us? And all around us? Do we know their names? Have we heard their stories? Do we eat with them? In fact, Jesus at one point says that the way that the Son of Man came was eating and drinking (see Luke 7:34). God's strategy for the world changing was to go and have a meal in someone's house, proclaim peace in that place and then God could meet them. Jesus ate with people, listened to them and then met their needs. I wanted to meet and know my neighbors... but for many reasons I would drive in, park my car and go inside my house without putting action to my desire. I started to feel so much tension and even conviction from the Holy Spirit around this; I was bothered by it. I read the Scripture and taught others about loving their neighbor at church, but I didn't even know my own neighbors. In the midst of all my questions, one resource I really benefitted from was *The Art of Neighboring* by Dave Runyon and Jay Pathak.

WHAT WAS ONE OF THE MOST CHALLENGING ASPECTS ABOUT ACTUALLY LOVING YOUR NEIGHBORS AS YOURSELF?

J: We'd been praying for six months for God to open a door to connecting with our neighbors, and something wild happened while Adam was out of town on a ministry trip. As I was pulling into my driveway, I saw a mom with her little girl and a friend walking from my yard. I'd never seen them before. I asked, "Can I help you?" The woman said, "I'm here to enroll my daughter in your Day Care." I replied, "Uh, I don't have a Day Care." "But I see all the kids here all the time," she answered. I laughed, "Oh, those are just my neighbor's kids. They just play here." We exchanged names, she left and I didn't think anything about it. The next day I was driving home again, and she is back with four other kids just playing in my yard! I thought, *This is strange, but I guess kind of cool?* We talked, met the kids and then I just went in my house. *I'm not sure what's happening here, but I guess they can play here. It's not a big deal.* The next day, there were fifteen kids in my yard, and they weren't just little kids anymore; there were several teenagers who ended up hanging out at my house the entire day.

I quickly called Adam, "I am freaking out. Maybe this is God answering our prayers, but I don't know if I want this." Adam and I talked, and I decided to actually engage all these strangers. The next day I had a utility man come to the house to do some work, and the atmosphere of kids running around my yard was pretty crazy. He came in the house at one point and asked me, "Did the city put a park in your yard? I just counted twenty-eight children out there." Was I really okay to have my neighbors at my house all the time? This was the first challenge on our journey for us to learn every kid's name who came to play. We started listening to their stories and not presuming anything about who they were, what they'd gone through. I just started having simple conversations, "You are welcome here at our house. What's your name? My name's Juli." It was really hard. It opened up a discussion for our whole missional community about what we're really saying when we claim we're willing to love our neighbors. The bottom line was, it made us all think, *How will that inconvenience me?*

A: Fast forward a couple of months, and now we were interacting with the kids on a first name basis. There was no more driving in and driving out anymore, no more being wrapped up in my own world. I started really enjoying the kids. Near our neighborhood, there's this big, open field. My imagination ran wild with fun ideas for what we could do with the kids in that field. I talked to our other friends about hosting a Neighborhood Camp. We planned and prayed for a couple of months. I remember knocking on doors around the neighborhood with my girls, saying, "Hey, we're doing a Neighborhood Camp. Would you like to send your kids?" The first household I went to, the mom just said, "Yeah, you can take my kid now!" So, her little boy just came walking with us and other kids joined in as I walked around recruiting campers. The kids started proposing new kids to invite, "You gotta go to this kid's house! And this one!" We finally held our first ever Legacy East Camp, and it was the most fun thing we've ever done. We put a massive slip-n'-slide in the field, Chick-Fil-A donated food for everyone and we talked together about a Father who loves us. It was the best three days. At the very end, we told the kids, "We'll be back here next Friday for a Neighborhood Night! We'll play kickball and eat. Whoever wants to come, come." And in three days, thirty kids showed up. It was wild what the Lord did!

Photograph by **JEFF JONES**

WHAT ARE YOUR RELATIONSHIPS LIKE WITH YOUR NEIGHBORS THESE DAYS NOW THAT YOU'RE FOUR YEARS IN?

J: Just by praying, God used something so simple, like us being present to the kids in our neighborhood, to open our hearts. He showed us what we really believe, and who to love, and how to love. Two years later, we had another utility man at our house working, and there were eighteen kids at our house that day. He asked me the same question, "Who are all these children?" In that moment I realized the journey that the Lord had taken us on, because my response was: "Well, that kid over there, his name is this, and he lives just across the street. This is his story. And that kid over there, this is her name and she lives three doors down, and this is her story." They had become my friends. Now I referred to my real neighbors as my real friends. That's the beauty of what happens when we love our neighbors as ourselves—we gain friends. We don't just become good neighbors, we become God's family. We've been loved and cared for by our neighbors way more than we've loved them!

A: We met one of our neighbors right after a bunch of teenagers nearby had broken into our house. It ended up being relatively harmless, but it caused one of our neighbors (a Vietnam veteran) to watch over our home from that day forward. His mom had taught him as a boy that everything he could see from his front door was his responsibility to protect with his life. So, he started patrolling our house to protect us. Isn't it amazing that we met one of our neighbors in a moment of vulnerability? As Christians, we often think we're going to be good neighbors to others. Meanwhile, we're not prepared to be met in *our* need. Being a neighbor means being okay with your own vulnerability, being a person in need—not the one who brings the solution or answer. It caused me to think, *Am I okay with others helping me and my family?*

There was another family that moved into our neighborhood with three teenagers. They've become so dear to us now. Their mom invited us over to her house for a meal, and we'd barely been invited to anything by our neighbors at this point. In that moment, I saw our neighbor showing us how to be hospitable. Before we even asked them, they were the ones who said, "Can you come eat with us?" At dinner, the mom shared with us her story; I was blown away by her vulnerability. So many things have transpired from this one relationship forming. If we listen to each other and swallow our pride, I'm learning, often our neighbors are the ones teaching us. It's such an incredible give-and-take relationship.

CAN YOU TELL US A BIT ABOUT THE BLESS MODEL?

A: The BLESS Model is something we've beautifully adopted. It stands for B-Begin in prayer, L-Listen, E-Eat, S-Serve, S-Story. For our Neighborhood Nights, once a week we eat something simple outside on tarps or picnic blankets in the middle of the apartment complex. We realize our humanity together when we eat at the same table; it is the great equalizer. Eating can just be as simple as barbecue outside if you're not comfortable eating in each other's homes. And eventually someone says, "I need help with this." Or you choose to ask for help. And you help each other, and you grow your relationships. Then stories are told at a deeper level. We can't tell our story without sharing the One who helps us everyday, the One who helps us with our kids. The One who helps us not worry about things. We share where we need help from God. Then God becomes part of our everyday lives with each other, and He gets the credit for everything.

That's been our journey over fifteen years—going from isolation to God creating the art of neighboring. We have struggled with our own attitudes and questioned whether anything good was happening in our neighborhood, but when we look back, we know God answered our prayers. He wants to bless every family on Earth, so our dream is to teach the Church how to bless. God is the center of it all—life and relationships. It's not just people being good to each other. We believe that in twenty years there will be a legacy in Legacy East.

J: Last summer, when we did our Neighborhood Nights, this local magazine approached one of our neighbors. This magazine writer wanted to show the diversity of Kansas City, how different the various parts of town were. Our friend said, "If you want to know my neighborhood, then you need to come to our Neighborhood Nights." This writer came from a wealthier neighborhood, and he was blown away, "I've never seen this. I wish I lived in your neighborhood, where people know each other's names and know the simple joy of being together." It was so awesome for us to see him respond that way. He was touched by seeing neighbors come together instead of being isolated. It showed the fruit of the years we'd been practicing the BLESS Model.

WHAT FINAL PIECE OF ENCOURAGEMENT DO YOU HAVE FOR US TO ENGAGE OUR NEIGHBORS WHOLEHEARTEDLY?

A: Neighbors are where we work, play, study—not just where we live. We all have overly busy lives. Capacity is usually the excuse we use to avoid our neighbors. I think at first, neighboring feels like something that takes away from us. We don't realize it's actually something that adds to our lives. There's always a blessing in doing what Jesus taught us. As we've taught families how to do this in very different contexts (i.e. cultures, socioeconomic backgrounds, stages of life, etc.), we've heard a lot of significant stories that are all about building connection and breaking down barriers. That is what happens when you listen, when you eat and pray together, when you offer help and receive help. Miracles start with simple meetings. If you never meet anyone, how do you know if a miracle is going to happen? Let's take the first step and meet someone. Then let God do what God does—miracles!

THE FRUIT LADY

by CHERIE BOLZ
photograph by MORGAN CAMPBELL

A few years ago, my husband Shawn and I were planning to move out of our house so our family could have more space. We lived up on a hill without much of a lawn, unless you call a cement patio on the edge of death for little toddlers a yard! In the middle of our busy lives with family, ministry and a million other things, I began to look for rental houses in Los Angeles. Sadly, I found that the whole inventory of the city was limited for a young family in regard to expanding our yard space. I randomly found one house that was like a diamond in the rough, except I knew my husband would only see the rough parts. It was a sweet little cottage on an acre of land in the middle of the valley, and it even had a cute little playhouse for our girls. I dragged Shawn along to go see it. While we were there looking through the property the owner came over. She was from Eastern Europe and began to ask us a lot of questions. I told her that we were in ministry and explained our life to her a little bit. She asked us about our faith more, and it seemed really significant that she was so open to talk about Jesus but was of a different religion. We said our goodbyes and carried on with life.

In the following weeks, however, I couldn't get her out of my head. I kept bringing her and the house up to Shawn: "Are you open to calling her and seeing if we could talk to her more about God? Or even praying for her?" He was on board, so we gave her a call. We held the phone as it was ringing; I was nervous. What were we going to say? I asked Shawn, "Are you getting anything?"—meaning, "Is God showing you anything for her?" He looked nervous, too, but all he said was, "Yes…" When she answered on the other line, she was very receptive to our call. She said she couldn't stop thinking about us either; she loved that we wanted to call. We started a wonderful conversation. She was easy to care about because she really is a beautiful person. I said, "Would you mind if my husband and I prayed with you?" She was very open, so I began to boldly pray. Then Shawn prayed, "I have this picture in my heart of you as a fruit lady. What does that mean?" She laughed, "I had no experience as a farmer, but I decided to buy an organic fruit farm. Everyone calls me the fruit lady, because I am so successful in growing my fruit!" Shawn said out loud a number and road name; he asked, "What is this address?" She said in surprise, "That is where my house and farm are! How do you know this?" Shawn said, "Jesus knows you and loves you. He is showing me that He wants to help you." This beautiful woman was going to have to look at God in a different way after us, because He came in real time through us and talked to her, sharing things we would've never known except through God!

This moment was incredible. In our busy world, God reached inside of our time and set some aside for love. He used my very real need and desire for a new house to meet with this lady of another faith; He gave me the courage and capacity to press into what could have been a very normal moment and transformed it into a divine one. Oftentimes we think we have to go, pursue, reach out with love and do something outside of our normal for God to have real space in our lives; but I'm learning that as a mother, wife, ministry leader and business owner, God can reach into my ordinary capacity and do beautiful things!

Prompt: Look at the seemingly normal parts of your life, and ask God to come within those spaces. Surrender your normal to Him, and let Him occupy your journey with His presence of love. Journal His thoughts about your daily life. Let Him turn any of your mustard seeds of compassion into His sovereign love for others. Be bold with sharing your heart for others, even if they are strangers who happen to cross your path; it just might change everything.

A WAR of BLESSING

by MARTHA MCRAE

It was a warm summer afternoon. I was sitting in my living room opening the day's mail. I sifted through bills, advertisements, a reminder from my optometrist office about an upcoming eye exam and finally reached a small package with no return address. It's rare that I receive unexpected packages, but getting mail is absolutely one of my favorite things, so I excitedly reached for the box and carefully slipped my finger underneath the tape-release seal.

My anticipation growing by the second, I lifted the flaps of the box revealing bright green and pink tissue paper. Wrapped inside were bags of my favorite tea, a small jar of local honey, a tube of chapstick, a gift card to a nearby coffee shop and a small envelope with ten dollars inside. I sat there in disbelief. The "war" money was back in my hands, and I had completely been fooled. She was sneaky beyond belief, and immediately I started scheming up a comeback.

Almost a year prior to this, I had given my neighbor Tiffany a dozen eggs and tucked ten dollars inside the carton to reimburse her for something she had picked up for me on a trip to town. While she cooked her eggs the next morning, she found the bill and insisted that I take it back. I will state here that I have an extremely strong stubborn streak that is most likely the result of growing up with a competitive older brother and working on a farm. When I refused to take the money back, she jokingly informed me that she believed her stubborn side to be equal to or larger than mine. Now, I know it's only ten dollars and you may be thinking, *Just take the money back. It's not a big deal.* It's true, the money wasn't a big deal, but more than anything I felt the invitation to be a blessing to my friend. Over the next couple of weeks we came to the understanding that neither of us were going to actually take the money. In playful stubbornness, together we declared a "war of blessing" on each other.

In the months to come, we would pass the money back and forth many times, accompanied by a handwritten note of encouragement, a trinket box, a beautiful mug, a bucket of local blackberries, handmade stationery, returned Tupperware, a bakery box with a cinnamon roll. It became a game of hiding it in each other's houses, trying to get it past the other person. We agreed that when either of us found the money that we'd acknowledge receiving it. Each of us would await the other's next move while we planned the pitch back. To this day (almost three years later) we are still sending it back and forth.

The fruit of this war has been connection, listening to each other's hearts, digging deep in thoughtfulness. No matter how small the gift, we know the gesture will bless the other person. The agreed value in our friendship is joy, and this simple game has mirrored the Lord's love to me. The Lord doesn't play games, but He is playful and does lead us with delight. The game has required us both to be intentional with our finances. Even on a tight budget, I've chosen to make it a priority to buy gifts I know will bless Tiffany. Every time I choose to buy that cup of coffee or a beautiful scarf, I am choosing to joyfully give of my finances.

Being wealthy or rich is not a prerequisite of being financially generous. Take the story of the Widow's Mite in Luke 21. This woman gave what she had—two small copper coins that amounted to one cent. Her giving was a sacrifice, but because of that Jesus honored her. He said that she contributed more than all the rest to the temple treasury. Others gave out of their excess, but she had given from her poverty. She didn't wait to sow in until she had plenty and it was comfortable for her to do so. How often do you let the belief that "there isn't enough" hinder your generosity? In these moments, you can choose to be led by fear or to be led by trust. I have encountered the playful side of the Lord that engages generosity as a joyful exchange, instead of an obligation. It is this understanding that inspires me to engage giving with excitement, knowing that God is never in lack and is always looking for excuses to bless His children.

PROMPT: How often have you seen generosity as an obligation rather than a joyful exchange? Practice repentance by trading the fear of "not having enough" for trust; exchange obligation for joy.

PRACTICE: Ask the Father for inspiration: "Lord, how can I practice generosity by financially blessing a friend?" This could be treating them to a simple cup of coffee, bringing a meal over or buying them a bouquet of flowers. Starting small is a great way to cultivate the value of generosity while partnering with Heaven to bless those around you.

> "WE ESCAPED LIKE A BIRD FROM A HUNTER'S TRAP. THE TRAP IS BROKEN, AND WE ARE FREE!"
> PSALM 124:7

ABOUT

The Cageless Birds is a community of leaders and artisans from Sophia, North Carolina founded by Jonathan and Melissa Helser. We are drawn together by an authentic passion for the Gospel of Jesus and a commitment to live out wholeness in community. We believe in the risk of saying yes to flying out of the cage of fear and soaring on the wings of true identity. We have fallen in love with pouring out our lives in ministry and then refilling our hearts in rhythms of family, friendship and creativity. This is sustainability. This is what it means to fly high and build home.

As leaders, we believe in and are committed to seeing a generation transformed by the Gospel. This commitment is walked out through our discipleship school, The 18 Inch Journey. Here, we set a table for students from around the world to come and encounter the love of the Father, the power of the Cross, the sustainability of the Holy Spirit and the beautiful transformation that happens in community.

As artisans, we come alive in creating goods throughout the year that help support our growing families and the mission of our schools. Whether it's creating music, writing books or cultivating one of our many other art forms, we are anchored with joy in the pursuit of excellence in all that we do. For more on the Cageless Birds, visit our website and online store at cagelessbirds.com.

2020 CONTRIBUTORS

THE CAGELESS BIRDS

JONATHAN DAVID HELSER
MELISSA HELSER
JUSTINA STEVENS
JAKE STEVENS
JD GRAVITT
ERIN GRAVITT
CHRIS MILLER
JESSIE MILLER
JOEL CASE
MOLLY SKAGGS
MARTHA MCRAE
ROSEMARY SKAGGS
LINDSAY VANCE
ZAC VANCE
ALLIE SAMPSON
PHYLLIS UNKEFER
SYDNEE MELA
MORGAN CAMPBELL
HANNAH HAYWORTH
JONO MACSORLEY
NIC FARLEY
ABIGAIL ROLLINS
CADE GARLOCK

FRIENDS OF THE CAGELESS BIRDS

TERESA ARCHER
Former Darling Magazine managing editor and author
Los Angeles, California | teresamarcher.com

SHAWN AND CHERIE BOLZ
Founders of Bolz Ministries
Los Angeles, California | bolzministries.com

ANDY BYRD
Leader of University of the Nations, YWAM Kona
Kona, Hawaii | ywam.org

ADAM AND JULI COX
Leaders of Eldership and Core Team of Navah Church KC
Kansas City, Missouri | navahchurchkc.com

JACOB DANIELS
Visual Artist and Owner of Common Good Co.
Boone, NC | overflowstudios.com

KALLEY HEILIGENTHAL
Worship leader at Bethel Church, songwriter for
Bethel Music, Pastor for BSSM
Redding, California | bethel.com

CASS LANGTON
Creative pastor and leader for Hillsong Church
Sydney, Australia | hillsong.com

MATT PETERSON
Lead Pastor of Awake Church, Founder of Hydrating Humanity
Winston-Salem, North Carolina | awakechurch.com

STEPHEN ROACH
Founder of The Breath & the Clay creative arts movement
Greensboro, North Carolina | stephenroach.org

LUCAS SANKEY
Photographer
Redding, California | lucassankey.com

LAUREN VALLOTTON
Director of Operations at Bethel Church
Redding, California | bethel.com

KAMRAN YARAEI
Author and Christian television host
Moravian Falls, North Carolina | ksministry.org

CREDITS

EDITOR-IN-CHIEF
Melissa Helser

ART DIRECTION AND GRAPHIC DESIGN
Melissa Helser, Justina Stevens,
Morgan Campbell, Lindsay Vance
& Nic Farley

COPY EDITORS
Courtney Clark, Teresa Archer,
Allie Sampson, Erin Gravitt,
Justina Stevens, Jessie Miller
& Phyllis Unkefer

PHOTO EDITORS
Morgan Campbell & Sydnee Mela

Cover photograph by Melissa Helser

Section Artwork by Jacob Daniels
& Justina Stevens

Handlettered titles & type by Justina Stevens,
Lindsay Vance, & Morgan Campbell

Hang gliding film photograph by Nic Farley

BIBLIOGRAPHY

[1] Vulnerability definition: "vulnerability." Dictionary.app. Apple dictionary, 2020.
[2] Scazzero, P., & Scazzero, G. (2017). *Emotionally Healthy Relationships: Discipleship that deeply changes your relationship with others: workbook: eight sessions.* Grand Rapids, MI: Zondervan.
[3] Passivity definition: "passivity." oed.com. New Oxford Dictionary, 2020.
[4] Bonhoeffer, D., Bloesch, D. W., Kelly, G. B., & Barnett, V. (2015). *Life Together.* Minneapolis: Fortress Press.
[5] Saint-Exupéry Antoine de. (2014). *The Little Prince.* Minneapolis: Graphic Universe.
[6] Eldredge, J., & Eldredge, S. (2011). *Love & War: Find your way to something beautiful in your marriage.* Colorado Springs, CO: WaterBrook Press.
[7] Bonhoeffer, D. (1958). The Cost of Discipleship. New York: Macmillan.
[8] Compare definition: "compare." Google.com Google, 2020.
[9] Augustine, Roberts, R. L., & Bigg, C. (1982). *The Confessions of Saint Augustine.* London: Mowbray.
[10] Extravagance definition: "extravagance." Google.com Google, 2020.

All definitions are quoted from the Merriam-Webster.com dictionary, 2020 unless otherwise noted.

Scripture reference from Opening Thoughts: John 10:27, ESV.
Section Break Scriptures: Proverbs 20:5, NIV; Ephesians 4:29, TPT; Proverbs 11:25, ESV.
About Scripture: Psalm 124:7, NLT.

All rights reserved, 2020.
No portion of this book may be reproduced
without permission from the Cageless Birds.

THE COLLECTION

Discover all the volumes of Cultivate at cagelessbirds.com.

I. THE HEAD TO HEART JOURNEY

An introduction to journaling with the Lord, featuring prompts and writings on topics from enjoying God and savoring your life, to freedom and identity. This book was created to help you establish rhythms of conversation with God.

II. THE CLARITY WINTER BRINGS

Designed to help you find beauty in quieter seasons of the heart, this book includes writings on topics such as hope, patience, perspective and stillness and is meant to encourage you to hear His voice in the midst of bare seasons.

III. FLY HIGH. BUILD HOME.

Created to bring understanding to what it means to live a sustainable life, this volume will explore what it means to thrive—to soar in the seemingly mundane moments of your life as well as the big-picture occasions.

IV. CREATIVITY UNLOCKED

Words and prompts that empower you to take risks in expression and discover your creative ability. These writings are meant to challenge your idea of what creativity is and unlock the truth that creativity is a birthright, not a skill-set.

V. THE ART OF CONNECTION, PT. I

Written with your most significant relationships in mind, Volume V is designed to encourage and empower you to pursue healthy and thriving relationships in dating, marriage, parenting and relating to your parents. May these writings inspire you with courage, hope and healthy perspective for God-centered relationships with those who mean the most to you.

VI. THE ART OF CONNECTION, PT. II

Centered around core themes of self-awareness, communication and generosity, Volume VI is designed to inspire transformative conversations with the Lord and propel you toward powerful, healthy relationships in every area of your life. It offers practical tools for how to maintain healthy connection with close friends, team, co-workers, acquaintances and strangers.

CONNECT + SUPPORT

TO PURCHASE COPIES
and other Cageless Birds goods
go to cagelessbirds.com or amazon.com

INSTAGRAM
@cagelessbirds

DISCIPLESHIP RETREATS
AND SCHOOLS
18inchjourney.com

WHOLESALE AND QUESTIONS
cagelessbirdsstore@gmail.com